MW00779576

Living the Paradox of Enlightenment

Spiritual Awakening in Simple, Clear English

by Thomas Razzeto

First Edition – November 2013
Second Edition – April 2017
Revised July 2021. Slight edits for greater clarity.

Paperback ISBN: 978-0-9826563-4-1

An Amazon Kindle edition is also available:
Kindle ISBN: 978-0-9826563-5-8

Thomas Razzeto was responsible for every aspect of
creating this book including all of the following:

Writing, except the foreword and quotations
Editing
Book design
Photography for the front cover
Front and back cover design

Timothy Conway wrote the foreword and his weekly
satsangs were invaluable in providing me with a solid
understanding of much of this ancient wisdom.

Dedicated to my dear father, who passed away in the fall of 2012, and to my loving mother. The love of God still flows freely to me from both of them.

Table of Contents

Is this book a good match for you? Find out quickly and easily by reading the free essays on my website. Please note that these essays are not "teasers" since they cover the core ideas of this beautiful, ancient wisdom. If you like my essays, you will probably like my book.

An ebook is also available.

Foreword by Timothy Conway

An old saying in Zen has it that "no mouth is big enough to utter This."

Having presumed for over 30 years to publicly babble utterances about This – the glorious Open Awareness that is our Unborn True Nature, the all-transcending yet all-embracing Reality – i am very, very happy to hear Truth being articulated in a clear and often quite unique way by "another mouth."

Over 20 years ago i had the pleasure to first meet Thomas Razzeto (in this lifetime anyway), and regularly for the last eight years have enjoyed his delightful presence at our weekly satsang meetings. ("Satsang" means "Divine assembly" or "association in Truth.") Thomas' voice in the book you are holding is transparent for who i know him to be on the personal level: a true *gentleman* (in the old Daoist and Confucian sense) – a living presence of loving-kindness, compassion, simple joy, and quietly deep (boundless!) openness.

In this gem of a book, *Living the Paradox of Enlightenment*, Thomas in his ever-friendly, brotherly way has generously shared a wealth of insights on how "your" life can be opened to the One Life underlying all lives – the Pure Awareness that is Source and Witness for all personal consciousnesses. This is the awesome Power of Reality that is *doing everything* and *being everyone*, the One Spirit Who is manifesting and animating all souls, the One Self of all selves.

One of the aspects of this book that I really commend and recommend is that Thomas has not just integrated and presented the nondual perspective and teachings about the One True Self (Absolute Awareness) based on the core teachings of our ongoing satsangs, and the crucial importance of a spiritually sane balance of deconstructive wisdom and empathetic compassion, but that he has also explored with readers how this all works vis-à-vis conditioned belief systems and relative viewpoints. Along this line, his short but rich chapters 1 through 5 are alone worth the (inexpensive) price of the book. And Chapter 6, about one of Thomas' own profoundly deep awakenings during a wrenching experience of loss, shows how this works even in dramatic, difficult circumstances. Subsequent chapters explore all of this more fully, continuing his adept use of illustrative stories and choice metaphors.

In these ways, his book serves as a very useful "wake up call" to help you, the reader, live from a much vaster Reality than what you might have thought was "real." Thomas has wisely seen through the illusions of the narrow, unsatisfying self-sense. He shows how certain belief-systems can confuse people and stunt their outlook. And he knows the delicious paradoxes that pertain upon awakening from the narrow "me-dream" to the wide-open Truth of our real Being, such as the grand paradox that we are *fully Divine* as the lucidly clear Essential Self while also expressing as the *fully human* in our current, poignant manifestation as the personal consciousness associated with the mortal body-mind. He knows that we are, in fact, the One adventuring as the Many, the Unlimited Reality playing with apparent limitations in the vividly-experienced "relative reality" (the dream-like, space-time play of material-mental phenomena).

With a sense of the serendipity of all this, Thomas invites you to investigate for yourself what's really right HERE (closer than the body-mind), right NOW (before you can even think about it), and how this Truth can beautifully manifest within a given life. He clears up a number of rampant misunderstandings and "half-truths" parading in our society as "spirituality" but which ultimately bring only confusion, frustration, and/or stagnation if one remains entangled in these positions.

So please consider well the insights presented by Thomas. They can serve as a lovely light helping illumine your own direct contemplation of real Truth, the Truth of Spirit discovered by authentic sages.

Verily, "this Truth shall set you free" into Your Innate Freedom.

Bowing directionlessly to Thy Infinite Nature

 – Timothy Conway

Enlightened-Spirituality.org

October 2013

Chapter 1 – Introduction

In this book, we will focus on enlightenment, personal peace and conscious creation. Or to put it another way:

1) Recognizing intuitively that you exist fundamentally as pure awareness, as the open capacity for experience.
2) Developing the ability to unselfishly flow in harmony with all that life brings forth.
3) Removing any unnecessary limiting beliefs that you might have about yourself, the world, and how you fit into it.

Let's briefly touch on these subjects right now.

Enlightenment

In 2005, I attended one of Timothy Conway's satsangs (meetings in Truth) in Santa Barbara. This was the first time I had ever heard anyone tell me that my fundamental self was pure awareness and that this awareness is the One Awareness, the Divine Awareness. This is what you really are when stripped of everything that is not essential.

I greeted this potentially huge shift in my understanding by only thinking, "Hmm, this sounds like very deep wisdom. I think I'll come back next week to hear more."

I had been on a spiritual path all my life and various people and channeled entities had been telling me for many years that I was divine, but this was the first time anyone had told me *how* I was divine.

Notice that my initial reaction to hearing this wisdom was not "Wow, this is fantastic!" Why? Simply because I did not yet understand it, both mentally and intuitively. It was only much later that I exclaimed, "Oh, now I see!" So don't feel left out if you don't "get" this material when you first hear it. Spend some time really pondering it. Sincerely ask yourself "How is this true?" rather than taking the usual approach of looking for reasons why it does not seem to be true. For whatever reason, this material usually takes some time to sink in.

Timothy's satsang presentations are extremely clear for two reasons: his own direct experiencing from age 16 onward, and his extensive study of all the ancient texts, which has been going on for over forty years.

Timothy can easily put this material on the table without making the room feel like a formal or rigid classroom and yet he primarily wants us to dig directly into our own experience. I will also encourage you to explore the true nature of reality in this way. You do not have to believe an authority figure since you can check this out for yourself. Reality, as always, is the supreme teacher.

Timothy's focus is always razor sharp: *the correct understanding of your True Self as pure Awareness is paramount. Being clear about that is the doorway to true liberation.*

Since I use this word "awareness" so often, I want to be clear about what it means. It just means the power of sentience, the capacity to perceive. Simple. Nothing new or surprising there, right? And yet your awareness is not just fundamentally who you are, it is also the Source of all of creation, the Source of all experience. This is why Timothy and I refer to this Awareness as "Source-Awareness."

By the way, it is also important to point out that this wisdom makes a distinction between Awareness and consciousness. Few people today make this distinction yet it provides the key to understanding how the One comes forth as the many. But we can wait until Chapter 9 to talk more about that.

So like Timothy, I passionately want to help you wake up to your True Self as the One Divine Awareness. This is the One Self that is arising as all "apparent selves," as each and every person. We will spend plenty of time exploring this fascinating subject.

Personal Peace

The second focal point of this book is the development of the ability to unselfishly flow in harmony and joy with all that life brings forth. You will become more skillful in the art of love and acceptance and in doing so, you will more easily experience a deep and lasting personal peace.

As your trust in God grows, you will discover that peace and joy are always available to you, no matter what your circumstances are. This recognition gives you the freedom to comfortably put your values of caring and sharing into action with a spontaneous aliveness that you have not known before. How beautiful is that?

Yet you were not created to just sit still in a peaceful state of acceptance. You are here to joyfully and fearlessly live your life in your own unique way, with kindness and compassion for everyone. This is why the creative process through which your life unfolds is the third focal point of this book.

Conscious Creation

Seth, as channeled by Jane Roberts, adamantly proclaims, "You make your own reality. There is no other rule." In a general sense, you (as a soul) can incarnate in every way imaginable yet you have chosen a certain theme to explore in this life. It is important to note that all themes offer joy, significant soul growth and greater wisdom. So don't worry about being trapped in a life full of suffering.

Also note that the popular claim that you can "be, do and have anything you want" (in this lifetime) is simply not true. The universe is not your personal mail order catalog simply waiting for you to clearly make up your mind and place your order, as you may have heard. But you can be happy without getting *everything* you want, right?

Conscious creation is not difficult to understand and it is easy to put into practice. The guidance of Chapter 11 will help you improve your life in significant ways.

Please note that these three subjects require a flexible presentation. While certain sections of the book do focus on one subject or the other, they are all connected so I will touch on all three subjects throughout the book.

Why Do We Call It Nondual Wisdom?

Since this wisdom is often called "nondual wisdom," we should take a few minutes to talk about what that means. "Nondual" means "not two" and we use it here because God and creation are seen as One Reality, not two. This is the deepest core idea pointed to by this wisdom and we say this because the unseen Creator *arises as* the creation we see all around us. This is very much like an actor arising as a character so let's go into this metaphor a little more.

Let's start by thinking of a Hollywood actor. Here it's easy to see that the actor is the source of the character. Surely it's not the other way around. The character is not the source of the actor. Furthermore, the character cannot go on the stage without the actor. And yet, the actor can drop the role of the character at any time. Because of this, it is wise to make a distinction between the *transcendent source* (the actor) and the *dependent construction* (the character).

And yet *when* the actor comes forward as the character, they are one. If you are standing in front of the character and you want to find the actor, you do not need to dig into a deeper and deeper layer. No. When you look into the eyes of the character, you are looking directly into the eyes of the actor. They are one.

Every single quality or aspect of the character is truly a quality or aspect that is being exhibited by the actor, and every single action that appears to be done by the character is really done by the actor. What appears to be the will and power of the character are really the will and power of the actor. *The character is not the source of anything and has no substance of its own.*

Of course you see what this metaphor is pointing to. God is the one *invisible* Actor who is coming forward as each and every *visible* character, as each and every *visible* person. All of creation is a spontaneous emanation that comes about when formless Source-Awareness (God) miraculously and paradoxically appears as the form that makes up not only our own physical world, but also all of our spiritual worlds. Ice doesn't just come *from* the water, it *is* the water, and so it is with God and creation. God is not only infinitely intimate with all of creation, God *is* creation.

So even though God and creation are not separate, we still make a distinction between the *transcendent source* (God) and the *dependent construction* (creation). The word "nondual" points to both this unity and this distinction.

If we constantly focus on the "Oneness" of everything, we might overlook some of the differences between people and things that we need to acknowledge in order to function well in the world. And yet to operate in the world without the recognition of the One Essence of all things would miss the big picture. This is what opens up the loving heart of enlightenment, so you see why it is so important.

Duality

Now let's consider the concept of duality, which brings to mind examples such as hot and cold, male and female, and the two sides of one coin. These examples demonstrate the three ways that duality can be expressed in our world. Obviously the coin has two sides and both sides must be present at all times. Gender, on the other hand, shows up for each person as either a male body or a female body, so this is quite different from the coin. And hot and cold demonstrate a third type of dualistic expression since temperature shows up anywhere along a continuum between two opposite polarities.

These three examples all exist in our physical world but there are also emotional dualistic pairs, such as happiness and sadness, and frustration and satisfaction. Yet no matter what, duality is always expressed in one of these three ways: as one thing with two inseparable parts, as two complementary aspects seen one at a time, and as something in-between two polarities. The ancient nondual texts call all of this "the play of the opposites."

Are "tree" and "non-tree" a well-matched dualistic pair?

I prefer to say that our world contains many dualistic expressions rather than saying that the world itself is dualistic or that everything in our world has a dualistic complement. For example, I don't think it's helpful to wonder what the dualistic complement of a tree could be, although some people do pursue this. They suggest that it is "non-tree" but I don't see how this completes a well-matched dualistic pair. Let's look into this a bit more.

While a tree exists as an object in our physical world, "non-tree" does not exists in the physical world. It is a concept and as such, it exists only as a thought within our minds.

This is why I don't think "tree" and "non-tree" make a very well-matched dualistic pair.

All the dualistic pairs that ring true for me have both aspects in the same realm. Hot and cold are both physical, while happiness and sadness are both emotional. So "tree" (a physical object) and "non-tree" (a concept) seem poorly matched to me. But notice that phrases such as "this is not a tree" or "not this tree" can still be quite useful.

In a similar way, the concept of "not me" is helpful in the process of disidentification, which I talk about in Chapter 9. But the point I want to make here is that "me" and "not me" are also not a well-matched dualistic pair since you are not a concept but "not me" is a concept.

Multiplicity

Now, when it comes to trees, they are all unique so the concept of multiplicity is more applicable than the concept of duality. The same thing can be said about everything – cars, houses, rivers, mountains and so forth. People are certainly unique so the concept of multiplicity is again very helpful. Obviously to function in the world, we need to distinguish between all the important qualities that make people and things different.

Here's a very short story to help underline this point. Imagine that you go out for breakfast and order some oatmeal. Minutes later your food arrives but instead of oatmeal, you receive a bowl of sawdust. You give the waiter a puzzled look and ask, "Hey, where's my oatmeal?" He just laughs and says, "Everything is God; sawdust is oatmeal." Not much help, eh? Just because everything has the same Divine Essence doesn't mean that everything is the same.

In form, we witness an endless display of differences but the whole story is that everything we experience is a unique and ever-changing expression of the One Divine Essence. This is why I like to say that our world contains both dualistic expressions and expressions of multiplicity and all of this is thoroughly divine without any exceptions at all.

Duality Is Not Something You Need to Deny

Please take careful note that the philosophy of nonduality does not say that dualistic expressions do not exist or that duality is not a helpful or valid concept. Instead, dualistic expressions, like all phenomena, are said to exist in our experience. They are experientially real since they can be witnessed. In our experience, hot and cold are real and different so it is wise to heed this experiential reality and not fall into any misunderstandings about that.

In my opinion, the correct understanding is that dualistic expressions themselves are not the cause of any trouble or dissatisfaction. Yet some dissatisfaction can arise if there is some emotional rejection of the conditions at hand. In the deepest way, dualistic expressions are not problematic precisely because they are all an expression of the One Divine Essence.

When dualistic expressions are correctly understood, you see that they are not a problem that you need to solve or overcome. But even so, you still might want to work on certain things to bring about what you prefer in an unselfish way.

Good and Bad

Now let's talk about good and bad and let's do so by continuing with the example of getting sawdust instead of oatmeal for breakfast. How would you feel about that?

Would you add a strong emotionally charged judgment to the mix? Perhaps. But most likely you wouldn't be too upset and instead, you would simply ask nicely for a bowl of oatmeal rather than sawdust.

Notice that you would not directly experience the bowl of sawdust as intrinsically bad. In your direct experience, you have simply received a bowl of sawdust, which is neither good nor bad but is instead completely neutral. It is only when you add to the mix your unmet desire for oatmeal followed by your emotionally charged judgment of dissatisfaction that you would then experience a "negative" emotion.

Now, I certainly think it is okay to have wholesome (unselfish) desires and preferences. Without desires, nothing would happen. But how you handle your unmet desires is the key. Notice that even if the situation is not what you want, saying so would not necessarily imply that you are not at peace with it. Saying that something is unwanted or "bad" can be done with or without a strong emotional charge, and obviously leaving out the emotional charge allows you to enjoy the peace that is available in every moment.

So when things become challenging, see if you can practice being at peace. This is often called "acceptance" but please let me clear up a common misunderstanding. This is very important. While it is wise to drop the emotionally charged pushback against "what is," it is also wise to actively work on making things better. Don't just sit in a "bad" situation and say, "Oh well, I guess this is all that God is going to give me." Calmly evaluate both your situation and what you can do about it. Don't just go hungry or eat the bowl of sawdust just because it's all you have. Instead, ask nicely for some oatmeal. I bet someone will gladly bring it to you. Maybe the first waiter will be pleased to see that you calmly adapted to his playful stunt.

When you learn to not cling to what we commonly call "good" in a needy way or push back with anxiety against what we commonly call "bad," you become free from dissatisfaction. The key is to assess things without these charged emotions. This allows you to emotionally accept things in a peaceful way while still working to make them better. I've heard this called "glowing with the flow" and I talk about it more in Chapter 10.

With this balanced attitude, you can now use words like "good" and "bad" in a helpful way. So our nondual wisdom does not forbid these words. Instead, it simply points out that we can remain at peace when we use them without any harsh judgment. In my opinion, this point is often misunderstood.

Always Work for the Good

Good and evil are the two polarities of the quality of morality. Of course people have forever debated the moral code, but even without settling that question in a way that will satisfy everyOne, good people are motivated in their own unique and wholesome way to do good things and work for a "better" world, as seen from their own perspective. They are fully engaged in life, offering loving kindness and compassion to everyOne, without being entangled in selfishness or self-centered desires. They are in the world but not trapped by it.

So paradoxically, even though our nondual wisdom advises us to emotionally accept what we commonly call "evil" without any harsh judgment, it does not in any way give us permission, so to speak, to harm others. As much as possible, in our own unique way, we always work for the good.

Some Additional Thoughts

I also want to mention that it is perfectly fine to speak from the perspective of our ordinary world and say things such as "I love you." Yet some people loudly protest that this statement presents a dualistic understanding and therefore should be thrown into the trash can.

Can you imagine a philosophy that forbids you from expressing your love for another person? Thankfully, the full nondual wisdom encourages these expressions of love since this is how the One Divine Essence shows kindness and compassion for those that are dear to us.

So we see that it is fine to speak from the perspective of either the One or the many. In fact, when it comes to getting things done in the world, speaking from your perspective as a person is an excellent way to be practical. What good is a philosophy if it prevents you from being practical?

By the way, when we speak of "the One Awareness," we are emphasizing the idea that this Awareness is always whole. It cannot be broken into pieces, whether those pieces are disconnected or connected. Nor can it branch out like the branches of a tree. This Awareness never has any divisions or parts yet through the mystery of creation, this One Formless Source-Awareness comes forth in our world of form as that which appears to be the many. How magnificent!

It is God who is arising as everyOne and it is God who is doing everything.

When we celebrate both our divine uniqueness in form and our divine unity as Source-Awareness, we find the deepest inspiration that opens up our loving hearts to everyOne. It is only through the many that we can share the One Love of God.

Since God is completely invisible, it looks like creation stands alone without any Creator at all. And yet, the Creator and the created are One! This is what our ancient nondual wisdom points to.

Nonduality: God and creation are One Reality, not two.

~ ~ ~ * ~ ~ ~

Will reading this book change your life? Well, if you calmly take your time without rushing and simply ponder the ideas that I present, you will have a very good chance of moving into a much deeper understanding of some of the most interesting questions about life and God. These are not difficult ideas at all, they are just very different from the way we normally think. That's why it might seem hard at first to understand them, but don't worry, it's really pretty simple.

Furthermore, I have carefully designed this book to stimulate an intuitive awakening within you. The next few chapters might seem overly simplistic but please bear with me. They lay the foundation for the later chapters and all chapters contain ideas that are worth pondering.

As this spiritual awakening deepens and your thinking becomes clearer, your mind and intuition will be able to work together in a very powerful way. Even still, all of this takes time to fully unfold so again, patience is important.

If you also put into practice the easy technique to change your core beliefs to allows you to enjoy a positive emotional state of being most of the time, you *will* change your life, perhaps dramatically.

So let's get started!

Chapter 2 – Is the World an Illusion?

We have all heard people say that the world is an illusion. But why would anyone say that? (Imagine the sound of bare knuckles knocking on a solid table: knock, knock, knock.) It sure seems real to me! But wait a minute. Does the apparent solidness of the world prove that it is not an illusion? No, it doesn't, and we will look into that point a little later.

But for right now, let's just look into the definition of an illusion. The dictionary says that an illusion is something that exists in a deceptive way. Yet it seems to me that many people mistakenly think of an illusion as something that does not exist at all. You hear this kind of thing all the time. For example, one minute someone will say that time is an illusion, and then the next minute, they'll say that time does not exist. But it must exist in order for it to be deceptive, in order for it to be an illusion.

Let's dig a little deeper into this subject by considering a stage magician. He's a master illusionist. Many people have seen the magic trick where he puts his assistant in a big box and cuts her in half with a saw. What we see is real. We see her head, arms and feet sticking out of the box. But we are not seeing the whole picture. Of course we all know that we don't see another person hiding in the box who makes up the other half of the assistant and this creates the illusion of one person cut into two pieces.

Even though our physical senses are doing their jobs perfectly, our incomplete picture seems to show that a false idea is true. Our incorrect assumption that the feet that we see are the feet of the assistant points to the false conclusion that the assistant was cut in half. Once we see the bigger picture, we understand the true nature of the situation and we no longer believe the false idea pointed to by the illusion.

But notice that there is something interesting about all good magic tricks. Even when we know the secret to the trick, if it is performed well, it still gives us the impression that something impossible just happened. So the illusion is persistent. Even though we are not tricked by the illusion in the deepest way, the false idea still appears as if it is true and this is why we enjoy the magic show.

Now let's consider the illusion of the movies. Even though the art form is called "the movies," you have never seen a single moving picture. Instead of true motion, many still pictures are displayed one at a time so rapidly that we perceive what seems to be moving images. And again, even when we know the truth, the illusion still persists. You always perceive what appears to be smooth motion even though this motion *does not exist objectively in the world*, it only exists subjectively. *It only exists in your experience.*

And notice the difference between the movies and the magic trick. With the magician, we knew we could not see into the box. That was an obvious limitation and it led to our investigation of what was being hidden from us. But with the movies, there is no obvious deficiency in our ability to perceive what is going on. So we don't question our experience or doubt the existence of the moving images. We might never wake up to the true reality of the situation unless someone tells us about it.

Now let's talk about the apparent motion of the sun traveling across the sky. This is an excellent example of a natural illusion, and these are the most important ones for us to understand. In this example, if you did not know any better, you might insist that the sun moves across the sky while the Earth remains perfectly still. That's what it seems like. You might even have precise measurements of the position of the sun at various times throughout the day and your records might go back for thousands of years.

If I showed up and told you that the sun does not move across the sky, you might reject my statement out of hand. After all, you have plenty of data that seems to prove otherwise. If I further explained that the earth is spinning on its axis, you might be cautiously intrigued. You might admit that if the earth were truly spinning, this would indeed create the *apparent* motion of the sun traveling across the sky, but you would also point out that that doesn't prove anything; it only presents a hypothetical possibility. And you would finally note that you should feel the earth spinning but you don't.

(Note: The sun does indeed move through space. The sun – along with the rest of the solar system – is orbiting around the center of the galaxy and one orbit takes about 250 million years. But the apparent motion of the sun traveling across the sky is due almost entirely to the spinning of the earth, not the motion of the sun traveling through space.)

Now, let's suppose that I take you out in a spaceship to a vantage point where you can clearly see the sun and the spinning earth. You would learn the true nature of the situation from personal experience. And yet, when you got back to earth, the illusion would persist. You would still see the sun *apparently* traveling across the sky! At noon, it would be high in the sky and about six hours later, it would be setting low in the west. And no matter how hard you tried, you would not be able to feel the spinning of the earth. Even though there really is something happening to you, you cannot feel it directly with your body.

When the subject of a spinning earth was first suggested to western culture in about 200 B.C. by Aristarchus of Samos (near Turkey), scholars presented several arguments against it. They claimed that people would be flung off the surface of the earth, and that birds would have to fly hundreds of miles per hour just to stay above one spot. It seemed like an impossible scenario and "common sense" prevailed in a way that defeated the truth of the matter.

If you wanted to be accepted by society, you could not endorse this new idea. If people thought you were a "nut," you would be passed over when it came to good jobs that carried a lot of responsibility or social status. And you certainly would not have been hired as an astronomer! But holding this false belief did not hinder anyone's daily activities and since people's fundamental desire to fit into society is so strong, the correct idea virtually disappeared from western culture.

In 1543, Copernicus reintroduced the idea that the earth spins on its axis as it orbits the sun, and again the idea got little support. Many people today believe that Copernicus waited until the end of his life to publish his ideas because he did not want the condemnation of the Church and the ridicule of his peers. During his time, those were the two most powerful forces motivating him (and everyone else) to just fit in.

Obviously these days, the Church does not play a dominant role in matters of science and astronomy; that role is now handled by the scientific academy. Yet getting on the "wrong" side of either of these forces will still present difficulties for "new" viewpoints that are worthy of proper consideration and more investigation. The power of ridicule continues to be very strong even though it is virtually overlooked as a force that shapes the beliefs of a society and therefore the beliefs of most individuals in that society.

But let's get back to our story.

Over 100 years later, Galileo provided conclusive evidence that Venus orbited the sun with his telescopic observations of the phases of Venus, which look similar to the phases of our moon. It was subsequently shown that all the planets orbit the sun, and that the earth spins on its axis. So finally, about eighteen hundred and fifty years after the idea was first presented to them, the western mainstream scientific community adopted the correct understanding. And notice that it did not just become socially acceptable to believe that the sun was the center of the solar system; it became a social requirement. Otherwise, you were pushed aside as a "nut," but this time for the opposite reason!

Incidentally, one way to prove that the earth is spinning is to construct a very large pendulum, say 200 feet tall, and set it in motion. As the day progresses and the earth spins, the section of the ground that the pendulum swings over will change significantly and this can easily be observed (except at the earth's equator). This was publicly demonstrated by the French physicist Leon Foucault in 1851 in Paris but it is fairly low-tech so it might have been done even earlier. But the main reason why western culture resisted investigating this subject for so long was because you cannot feel the spinning of the earth directly with your body.

The spinning of the earth provides an excellent example of how difficult it is for us to break free from incorrect beliefs **when these false beliefs are based on misleading personal experiences** <u>**that are shared by everyone**</u>. *Add to that the dynamics of peer pressure and the fundamental desire to be accepted by society and you see how easy it is to fall into the trap of an illusion.*

This point is especially important when it comes to understanding the True Self. There is only one self and that is this pure Source-Awareness. The combination of your body, mind, personality and soul can be called your "functional self" or your "personal self" but it is not really a self since it is not really an autonomous entity. It is not the source of what appears to be its own awareness, just like the moon is not the source of what appears to be its own light. Yet from the point of view of our common "ordinary" world, you will experience your functional self in a way that makes it seem as if it is the only real you, while seeming both separate and mortal. But this is just an illusion. The personal self is something that exists in a deceptive way.

A sage is both wise and practical. In our example of the spinning earth, it is wise to live with the understanding that the earth is spinning on its axis, and yet it is practical to speak about the sun as if it were truly traveling across the sky. For example, it is perfectly fine to ask your friend if they saw the sunset, which implies that the sun moves down out of view. You don't need to burden yourself by asking if they were outside looking west when the earth rotated in such a way that the horizon blocked the sun. While that is indeed the correct scenario, we don't need to worry about speaking that way. Our normal language works fine since that is what it looks like and everyone knows what we mean.

Similarly, we can relax about using "you," "me," "him," "her" and so forth when referring to ourselves and other people. If someone asks you if you went to the beach, you don't need to reply, "I am the formless Divine Awareness. I can go nowhere." That's a dysfunctional reply. While it is true, it's not helpful since it's not really what they were asking. We can tell from the context whether we are talking about the True Self or the personal self, and so we can continue to use our natural speech patterns without any problem.

Now, when it comes to the personal self, we won't suddenly declare, "Oh, that's not really me so I won't care about it at all anymore." That would be silly. We will of course behave responsibly and take care of our "selves" in a wholesome and practical way, without being selfish or self-centered.

The Apparent Solidness of the World

Now let's get back to the question of the apparent solidness of the world. I go into this more in a later chapter but I want to touch on it very briefly here.

Years ago I had a lucid dream where I was touching something that seemed to be solid metal. I was very aware that my experience of touching that metal in the dream was indistinguishable from my experience of touching solid metal in our ordinary world.

This fascinated me and I started to wonder, "If things in a dream can feel solid, could it also be true that our solid ordinary world is also a type of dream?" Obviously it's not exactly like a nighttime dream since it has continuity from one day to the next and it has other qualities that are much different from a nighttime dream. But could it still be a dream-like construction, an ever-changing fabricated story? And, like a dream, could our ordinary world also be an illusion? Could it exist in a deceptive way?

Some of this deceptiveness is revealed by out-of-body experiences (OOBEs), conscious memory of past lives and communication with spirits who have passed away. Yet OOBEs by themselves are enough to reveal that there is more to our world (and to us) than what we initially thought. Are we really only a body that is alive for a while and then gone forever? No, not at all!

While our magicians use ordinary means to create the illusion of a supernatural event, is God doing the opposite? Is God using supernatural means to create the illusion of the ordinary world? Yes! And I think most of us would probably not wake up to the truth of this matter unless someone told us about it.

The secret to understanding all illusions is understanding the bigger picture that holds the little picture, the illusion. It is important to note that the bigger picture does not invalidate the little picture. In other words, the little picture still offers a real and valid *experience.* Yet when we wake up to the bigger picture, we quickly give up the false idea that the illusion points to and we correct our understanding of the situation. But we don't ignore the experience of the little picture.

Notice that our lives are invigorated with genuine emotion precisely because we cannot perceive God in any way at all. Yet even when we wake up to the big picture, we become liberated in a joyful and loving way. We do not become uncaring, heartless or uninvolved, as some people seem to think. I will talk more about this in later chapters.

Before we go on to the next chapter, let's quickly consider the experience of time. I mentioned this subject at the beginning of the chapter and I just want to add a few thoughts. Could time also be an illusion?

Suppose you and your friends have plans for dinner and a movie, and you arrive promptly at the restaurant with your appetite piqued. But thirty minutes later, you are still alone and beginning to wonder if there was a misunderstanding. Is this the right day? Fifteen minutes later, you are just about to leave when your friends suddenly arrive.

Their apologies for being late seem a little disingenuous but you're willing to overlook that. They notice that you are a bit unhappy with the situation and they try to fix everything by proclaiming that you should not be so concerned about time since it is only an illusion, as if that means that it doesn't exist at all. But you might be thinking, "Hey, no matter what time really is, we're all having a late dinner and we're going to miss that great movie!"

Is time an illusion? Obviously our conventional approach allows us to coordinate our activities in a practical way so we shouldn't give that up. And you can't have growth without time, nor could you listen to music or see anything since sound and color are vibrations that unfold in time. But is there more to time than meets the eye? Does it exist in a deceptive way? I think so and this means that it's an illusion.

Perhaps I have inspired you to really spend some time thinking about these illusions. Now when you look up at the sun traveling across the sky, it will remind your that everything we experience is an illusion. All of creation is presented to us as a deceptive experience. All of creation is an illusion.

But what you truly are is not an illusion. You exist fundamentally as Source-Awareness, the only Reality that is not a thing, a transcendent Reality that witnesses (experiences) all of created reality.

With that in mind, let's move on to the next chapter.

Chapter 3 – Your Core Beliefs Create Your Perspective

This chapter will examine the often-overlooked factor of perspective, which is the vantage point from which you view our world. To get us started, let's consider one object seen by two people, you and me. Let's suppose that the object is shaped like a large, wide soup can and that I am above it looking down at its round top and suppose you are to the side and you see its profile as a perfect square. Let's also suppose that both you and I only understand the world as two-dimensional.

And I ask you, "Hey, do you see that object?"

"Of course," you reply. "It's a perfect square."

"A perfect square?" I protest. "How can you say that? It's a perfect circle!"

We could choose to have a big argument yet I know that you are my friend and that you are not trying to trick me. I also know that you have a pretty good handle on the world and that you have excellent eyesight. But I am puzzled as to how we can resolve our differences. After all, a square cannot be a circle, or can it? If the object is only one thing, shouldn't we both see it the same way? How can both of our experiences be valid?

Now suppose someone else enters the scene and explains to us that the world is really three-dimensional, not two. Ah ha! That's how we both can have perfect eyesight and yet see something completely different! In this way, an object can *appear to be* both a square and a circle, but not at the same time from the same vantage point. Of course, even with this new understanding, you will still see a square and I will still see a circle. That doesn't change. But if I shift my vantage point by moving next to you, I will then also see a square.

Okay, this is all very simple and obvious. Yet it seems to me that most people do not understand that *their unique collection of core beliefs creates their own unique vantage point from which they see the world.*

Because of this, everyone sees the world in their own unique way, sometimes in ways that are remarkably different. This is why there is so much disagreement about religion and politics, just to name two important areas. People roll their eyes and wonder, "How can the other group not see it my way? They must be completely blind or perhaps just stupid!"

But it has nothing to do with intelligence or the ability to perceive the world correctly; it all depends on the vantage point from which you observe the world and this vantage point is created by the beliefs you choose. This is why an IQ test given to the brightest priest and atheists will find high IQs in both groups. This is how one world can yield a wildly different experience for each and every person.

Now of course everyone says, "Hey, I only want to believe things that are indeed really true. Otherwise, I would just drop them!" But here's a key point:

Core beliefs are self-reinforcing in two important ways.

First, they impose a filter on how you see the world. For example, if you believe the world is a dangerous place, you will see many threats when you watch the news or talk to friends about the "bad things" that are happening to them and the people they know. There are threats from accidents, disease, criminals, severe weather and so forth. From this viewpoint, it certainly seems that the world is indeed a very dangerous place and this produces a constant state of fear that seems both justified and unavoidable. Anything that might support the idea of a safe world is simply overlooked or pushed aside since it is outweighed by what seems like so many obvious dangers.

The second way that your core beliefs are self-reinforcing is that they create experiences that confirm those beliefs. While this is happening to you on a personal level, you will also be inclined to spend time with other people who share your beliefs. In this way, everyone hears about all the validating experiences of anyone in the group. Because of this, everyone becomes absolutely convinced that their beliefs have been thoroughly examined and are most certainly correct, while missing the deeper understanding that their beliefs are a driving factor and can be changed.

I will talk much more about the creative process in another chapter but for right now, I just want to touch on it briefly.

Bashar (as channeled by Darryl Anka) points out that your beliefs, emotions and actions all work together to create your experience and your circumstances.

Your dynamic, in-the-moment thoughts about your ever-changing outer circumstances mix with your core beliefs to create your emotions. These emotions fuel your desire to act and you evaluate your options and pick the action that best fits your core beliefs. All of this leads to a fresh experience and a new set of circumstances. Working consciously with the process is not difficult unless you believe that it will be.

The process of creation is not about creating specific circumstances so that you can then choose to be happy. Instead, this is about learning to be happy first, and then working to make the changes that you prefer.

Most people ignore the first two parts of the creative process and just focus on action. This is like noticing in a mirror that your hair is messed up and trying to fix it by pushing a comb into the mirror. Nothing will change until you first change the core beliefs that are reflected outward.

All core beliefs tend to attract other similar beliefs and this process will create a cluster of beliefs, all focused on the central core belief. This happens for both individuals and groups. So if you hold a belief about the world being a dangerous place, you will soon attract more beliefs that fit that theme. At first, there might only be the fear of illness, but next you might adopt a fear of financial disaster and so on. As time goes on, this cluster of beliefs can become quite "massive," habitually accepted as true and automatically creating corresponding results. This is how core beliefs becomes so potent in their effect.

If there is a cluster of "negative" beliefs, it is important to deal with the core belief at the center of the cluster. When we dissolve that belief by recognizing that it only appears to be true and can be dropped, the entire cluster will fall apart.

Have you noticed that some people will actually come right out and bluntly tell you that a dark cloud follows them wherever they go? That is just one of their core beliefs. And yet other people greet each and every day with renewed joy, wonder and awe because they always feel like they are opening up presents on Christmas morning. They may not know specifically what is going to happen on that day, but they know that there will always be plenty to be happy about and with this joy also comes more love. That is their belief and it leads to their experience.

The dynamics between a group and the individuals in the group regarding their shared beliefs are too complex to go into here but surely you have noticed that some groups are easy to join yet difficult to leave. When it comes to religious and political groups, people often just stick to what they were born into. Beautiful, natural and strong interpersonal relationships are frequently built between family members and friends in a ways that use religion and politics as their foundation. Because of this, it may be difficult to give up key shared beliefs without giving up these genuinely satisfying relationships. So people often choose to leave their beliefs unexamined rather than risk exploring new beliefs that are not supported by these political and religious groups.

Regardless of any religious and political aspects, society as a whole also holds beliefs about how the world works and what it means to be human, and some of these beliefs do not serve us very well. If you push those beliefs aside, you often get pushed aside as a "nut." Peer pressure is very powerful; just look into some of the social psychology experiments about it. And it remains powerful because most people are uninterested in learning more about it. But when an individual is no longer afraid of the consequences of being different, peer pressure disappears. Will you be among the few who have the courage to do this?

Notice that both the beliefs and the system that helps keep the beliefs in place often continue without question.

The main point that I am making here is that when you don't look close enough, your unhelpful core beliefs will always seem to be correct, even though they can be replaced with new beliefs that are much more beneficial for you. This is why we will take the time in a later chapter to examine our core beliefs with a sharp eye. I was a bit surprised at what I found for me personally and perhaps you will have a similar experience.

Now let's move on to what I call the mystic's view.

Chapter 4 – The Mystic's View

Some people believe that God is in everything. How could this be true and yet not be obvious? How could a common rock contain the Creator? Let's look into this question by considering the following.

Suppose you have arrived on Earth from far away and are exploring it for the first time. And suppose you have found a block of frozen ice. As you examine the ice closely, you take note of its properties. It is so cold that it almost hurts to touch it. It is very hard and will not flow around your hand but if you hit it with a rock, you can break off a few pieces.

Then imagine that you discover a natural hot springs big enough to jump into. The hot water feels fantastic and you delight in how it flows all around your body. The water can be splashed about but it does not break into pieces.

Surely you have discovered two very different things, two things that have nothing in common at all. Their properties are exactly opposite. One is cold and solid; the other is hot and fluid. One is breakable; the other is not.

And then it happens. The block of ice falls into the hot pool of water and right before your very eyes, it melts in a matter of minutes. Now you clearly see that it is made out of the same thing that the hot water is made out of. There's no denying this now. But a few minutes ago it was very different. It was in a different form, a different state, which gave it a completely different set of properties, a completely different set of qualities.

Could this be similar to God and creation? Let's expand the water analogy by including water vapor, which is an invisible gas. That invisible gas might be like God the Source. We cannot see God the Source since the Source has no form. And yet, if the Source wanted to create a spiritual world, a world of angels, for example, the Source could choose to lower its temperature, its vibration, and "part" of the Source would change from an invisible gas into liquid water that now has a tangible form to it. This spiritual world could include beings with a sense of self and freewill. They would not appear to be the same as the Creator and yet they would be made out of the same divine essence. Beings in this world would have their senses tuned to that realm, that dimension, so they would be able to perceive and experience everything in it.

And if the Source wanted to create a physical world, to create our universe, the Source could choose to "lower the temperature" even more and "part" of the Source would then take on many magnificent new forms. Similar to before, this physical realm could also include beings with a sense of self and freewill. And again, they would not appear to be the same as the Creator and yet they would be made out of the same divine essence. These beings would, of course, have their senses tuned to the physical world allowing them to perceive and experience everything in it but they would generally be blind to everything in the spiritual world.

In this view, it's very important to note that while we are all made out of the same thing, we are not all the same. From the point of view of our common daily life, we each have our own unique "personal self," precious and special but not in an egotistical sense. We are each a unique expression of the eternal divine essence. We each have our own body, we each have our own personality and we each have our own thoughts and feelings. Yet while we are all different, we are all connected to each other, to everything, through this wondrous divine essence.

Now imagine for a moment that the eternal divine essence was wood. You can make a chair out of wood, you can make a house out of wood and you can make a boat out of wood. While all these things are made out of the same thing, they are each very different. If a storm is coming, the shelter of the house will benefit you the most, but if you are out on the ocean, the boat will serve you best.

So don't make the mistake of saying, "Well, since everything is divine in its essence, everything is the same in its form, and I will therefore not make any distinctions between people or things." Some people and things may mix with you in a more harmonious way so choose wisely and enrich your life!

And still, with this mystical understanding, you will perceive every act as a divine act, every thought as a divine thought, every emotion as a divine emotion and every thing as the divine in physical form.

In the formlessness of our divine Source nature, there is only oneness, wholeness, and yet, as such, nothing is manifest. It is here where we all dissolve into oneness. Yet in our physical world, this wholeness is presented to us in a way that makes everything appear to be separate, non-divine pieces. This is the false idea pointed to by the illusion of the world. But as I mentioned before, just because the world is an illusion does not mean that it is not real. It just means that it exists in a deceptive way.

Paradoxically, when the formless divine Source becomes manifest, it presents itself with form, with an appearance. It is this physical appearance that our scientists focus on and in many ways they do an excellent job. Yet few of them have any interest in the awareness that actually sees the world. Of course some of them study the physiology of perception but that is not the awareness. They also study what they call "states of consciousness" but all they are really studying are different states of the body and brain; they are not studying the invisible Awareness. This wondrous and divine Awareness is what you actually are.

This Divine Awareness is the buried treasure hidden within the "personal self;" it is the kingdom of heaven within you.

Your "personal self" appears to be your body, mind, and soul, but your True Self – your fundamental, unconstructed self – is this Divine Awareness that perceives everything that you experience. This is why I like to repeat an old saying:

"Know yourself and you shall know God."

Most analogies fall short in some respect and the water analogy is no exception, yet I like it in many ways. But is it true? Is everything we see actually the eternal divine essence in physical form? Is this divine essence at the core of the wonder and awe that we feel when we admire the beauty of nature and each other?

Mainstream science holds that the material qualities and chemical processes of the body and the brain give rise to our power of perception. In other words, the material world is the foundation of reality, and sentience is a byproduct that comes forth from specially organized matter, and this allows all sentient beings to be alive and aware.

But what if it's the other way around? What if your awareness is fundamental? What if your awareness is unconstructed and everything else is created within this?

Genuine in-depth scientific research into subjects such as out-of-body experiences, near-death experiences, spirit communication and past lives all point to a nature of reality that is profoundly different from the materialistic view of mainstream science. This research shows us that while there is a relationship between our personal consciousness and our body, the body is not the source of our consciousness. The true nature of the self goes beyond the body. Of course we all see that our bodies were born into the world; this is beyond dispute. But is it not also true that both our bodies and the entire world are "born" into our awareness?

Our amazing awareness itself is not even visible to us and yet we know it exists because we experience the world through it. Our awareness holds everything that we experience. Our awareness hosts our entire personal reality. Everything that you experience, physical or spiritual, arises "out of" your awareness and is witnessed by your unchanging awareness.

And the mystic carries this even further. A mystic understands that the awareness that looks out of your eyes is the same awareness that looks out of his or her eyes. What is seen is different but the awareness is the same. There is only One Awareness and this formless, unseen, Divine Awareness is what animates all of life.

Almost everyone is looking for a thrill. Most people are looking for the usual thrills such as great food and music, exciting vacations, a wonderful relationship with fabulous sensual experiences and so forth. Spiritual people may look for those things plus a transformational experience with a great teacher or a spiritual high at a sacred site.

While there is nothing wrong with those things, sometimes the desire for them becomes so strong that they virtually control the person's thoughts and actions. But the driven nature of those desires falls away when you realize that in your true nature, you are already complete. Now thrills can come and go without being urgently chased or tightly clutched. With this understanding, you are now satisfied with whatever arises.

Now let's have some fun with a 3-D dinosaur!

Chapter 5 – Can You See the 3-D Dinosaur?

In 1995, the first Magic Eye book was published. It contained many beautiful computer-generated images that at first appear to be only a meaningless jumble of colors without any recognizable objects. There are no trees, buildings, people or animals. Yet when you focus on an image in just the right way, suddenly you see a hidden 3-dimensional image pop right out of the page. The experience is quite unexpected and lots of fun. The book was so popular that several additional volumes were published and you can find more information on the Internet, including lots of examples and a few guidelines to help you see the images.

Due to copyright restrictions, I cannot put an example in this book but as I just mentioned, you can quickly find many on the Internet. I suggest you search for "magic eye 3-D dinosaur" (without the quotation marks) to see the image that I talk about in this chapter. With a little guidance and practice, most people are able to see the 3-dimensional dinosaur.

So why do I bring this up? Well, this reminds me of seeing the mystic's view, which, as we discussed in the last chapter, holds that God and creation are the same reality. I like to use the analogy of water and ice because ice does not just come *from* water; it *is* the water. Once you intuitively recognize the mystic's view, you accept it as true, even though you cannot logically prove it to other people since this comes about through a personal experience.

Similarly, if you have been able to see the dinosaur, even if only briefly, you know for sure that you have seen it; no one can convince you that it is not there. But if other people don't see it, they might think that you are imagining it. Let's explore this idea a little further.

Let's suppose that this image is over your city and it's so big that it fills the entire sky. Suppose that all throughout history, everyone thought that it was only a meaningless mass of colors without any recognizable figures. Then one day a little boy and girl look up and proclaim, "We see a dinosaur in the sky! We see a 3-D dinosaur!" They are brother and sister and their parents have no reason to think that the children would lie about this, but since no one else has ever seen this, well, the parents become concerned about their children's eyesight and take them to the eye doctor.

The doctor gives them every test in the book and the results are perfect. Not a speck of trouble anywhere. Then the parents and the doctors get the idea that maybe the reason other people don't see the image is that other people aren't looking for it carefully enough. So everyone starts to look for the dinosaur and, just to be sure, everyone gets their vision checked, but no luck. Only the two children are able to see this mysterious creature, which is now taking on mythic proportions.

Disappointed that they haven't been able to see the dinosaur themselves and frustrated that they haven't resolved the situation with their children, the parents now have the best psychiatrists come to evaluate the children. This brings both good news and bad news. The doctors find no indication of any personality disorders, but they conclude that the children are hallucinating. The logic seems as solid as a rock. No one else can see the image, yet the children say they see it. It must therefore exist only in their minds. But the children know the truth of the matter even though they have no way of logically proving it to anyone else since the proof comes in the form of a direct personal experience. All the children can do is repeat that the dinosaur is really there and encourage people not to give up trying to see it.

This example points out the difference between seeing something and recognizing it. Obviously, everyone that looks at the sky sees the same image and the dinosaur is always there. So in that sense, they see it. But only the people who look deeper into the image in just the right way recognize that the image contains the dinosaur. Everyone sees it but not everyone recognizes it. Likewise, everyone sees the physical world that is all around us but few people recognize it as our invisible Source-Awareness miraculously arising as all the visible objects of creation.

It is most common for people to look at the world with great interest while paying virtually no attention to their own awareness, which is what metaphorically holds all of these perceptions. As long as their awareness is "working" as expected, the focus is on the people, things, and events that are perceived, not on this power of sentience. Our attention is immediately off to where the action is in the exciting world around us. In this way, the profound nature of our awareness is overlooked, and the liberating treasure of recognizing what this awareness actually is escapes most people.

(By the way, your awareness is always working perfectly. It even accurately perceives the distorted images that arise due to alcohol, drugs or injury to the eyes. Similar things can be said about the other senses.)

Everyone knows that they are aware; this is self-evident. But similar to seeing but not recognizing the 3-D dinosaur, most people don't recognize that their pure awareness is their fundamental, unconstructed self. This is why I like to say:

You are not the sentient being you have considered yourself to be all your life. You are sentience itself!

Take some time to really think about existing in the most fundamental way as pure, open awareness, this open capacity for experience. Perhaps you will be able to focus deep enough in just the right way and recognize that this pure awareness is your true identity.

This is the awakening that the mystics have been talking about throughout the ages. So keep trying. Don't stop until the true nature of your fundamental self pops right out into your clear understanding, just like the 3-D dinosaur!

Chapter 6 – The Passing of Tookie Williams and My Experience with the Gift of Deep Sorrow

In late 2005, I became aware of a man on California's death row named Stanley "Tookie" Williams. He was scheduled to be put to death in mid-December and there was an effort to prevent this. By this time, Tookie had written or co-written about a dozen books which spoke out against gang violence and especially warned children about the false promise of gang life. His work was so influential that many people wrote him letters of gratitude. He was even nominated to receive a Nobel Peace Prize. Children and young teenagers wrote to say that only Tookie's work had kept them from joining a gang.

I did not know much about Tookie's past but I did know that he was one of the founding members of the Crips and had been involved in a very violent lifestyle, as you would expect from a man at the top of one of Los Angeles's most notorious gangs.

Yet his books, which he wrote while in prison, seemed to reveal that he was a changed man, with compassion and a strong desire to make the world a better place in ways that only someone who had been in the darkest shadows could. He could talk about gangs because he had been involved since he was twelve. He could connect with the black community of South Central Los Angeles because he was one of them. And by extrapolation, he could connect with people in other cities across the country and around the world.

In a December 2005 interview, with his probable death just hours away, Tookie said, "[Regarding] my lack of fear of this barbaric methodology of death, I rely upon my faith. It has nothing to do with machismo, with manhood, or with some pseudo former gang street code. This is pure faith, and predicated on my redemption. So, therefore, I just stand strong and continue to tell you, your audience, and the world that I am innocent, and yes, I have been a wretched person, but I have redeemed myself. And I say to you and all those who can listen and will listen that redemption is tailor-made for the wretched, and that's what I used to be. That's what I would like the world to remember [about] me. That's how I would like my legacy to be remembered – as a redemptive transition, something that I believe is not exclusive, just for the so-called sanctimonious, the elitists. And it is not predicated on color or race or social stratum or one's religious background. It's accessible for everybody. That's the beauty about it. And whether others choose to believe that I have redeemed myself or not, I worry not, because I know and God knows, and you can believe that all of the youths that I continue to help, they know, too. So with that, I am grateful. I say to you and everyone else, God bless. So take care."

I am not sure if I heard that specific interview but I did hear Tookie speak on the radio a few times that December and I imagine that he offered the same message each time he spoke.

His reference to being innocent stems from his claim that the charges that actually put him in prison were the result of being framed. Yet it cannot be denied that his past was filled with violence; this is beyond question.

The debate about whether Tookie had really changed did not matter much to me since in my view, he *was* a changed man. Most of Tookie's books were for children and often only about 25 pages long. In my view, these books were basically about peace and they were having a very positive effect on the lives of thousands of people. I am happy that Tookie was able to get these books into the hands that mattered most. In this way, he had become a force for good and his work was a priceless benefit to society.

So on the day the execution was supposed to take place, I could only hope that the governor of California would understand the immeasurable benefit of Tookie's excellent work and stop the execution. Just to be perfectly clear, it was not being asked that Tookie be set free, only that he be allowed to continue to live and work inside San Quentin State Prison. How could that be too much to ask?

It might be hard for me to convey in words all the beliefs that came into play for me that night. Was the state of California a heartless, cruel machine that just destroyed anything that seemed dangerous, even though this supposedly dangerous man was now completely disarmed? Were the forces of darkness so strong that peace was not even allowed to be discussed? Wasn't Tookie's track record of social benefit now obvious?

Over the course of several decades, I had learned about the death of President Kennedy and it seemed to me that the powers that pushed violence and war kept gaining more and more ground. My hopes and dreams from the Sixties for love and peace seemed to have evaporated right before my eyes. I had been working hard on my writing for over five years but that was not getting any attention. And yet here was Tookie, getting the job done beautifully! Surely he should be allowed to continue! In fact, the prison should be promoting his work throughout the entire country and beyond!

That night I went to bed around 11 PM and I knew that the execution was scheduled for midnight. I fell asleep not knowing what to expect. Inexplicably, I awoke a few minutes before 1 AM. I knew that the news would start at the top of the hour and that most likely, if I turned on my clock radio, a man would come on and tell me whether or not Tookie had been saved. I slowly but anxiously reached for the button, already very concerned since I had never heard of anything like this being prevented at the last minute. Sure enough, the lead story was about Tookie. A man just reported without emotion that Tookie was now gone, no longer available to help us all, and no longer there for his family and friends. I was crushed. The flood of emotions was much stronger than I could have expected. After all, this was a man I had never met and only heard on the radio for no more than an hour.

John Kennedy stood up tall for peace. He was struck down. Tookie Williams stood up tall for peace. He was struck down. What was going to happen to humanity's peace project? Could we really bring peace to the whole world, one person at a time? Was there really something that we could do to help make this happen or was I just holding false hope? If I stood up for peace high enough to be seen, would I, too, be pushed aside? Why had there been this senseless killing of such a beautiful person, this man of peace? Why? When the state of California executed Tookie, I felt as if this callous institution had crushed all the hope that I held for a better world. In fact, it was almost as if they had crushed me, all my work, and everything I dreamed about. Who was going to correct our "correctional" institutions? Who? And when?

My crying started immediately and it quickly became so deep that I didn't know anyone could cry that hard. The tears poured from my eyes like a dam had burst; my breathing had a staccato pulse and my voice could only send out the painful wail of my breaking heart. This was genuine human sadness at its deepest and it was natural. I certainly was not thinking, "If I were more spiritual, I would be happy all the time." No, this sadness flooded my experience in an overwhelming yet natural way, without any extra thoughts about what sadness should or should not be.

While I was crying, I had the thought that I wanted to know what this deep sadness really was. It seemed that it was as big as a mountain and as solid as a rock. It was simply massive. And I wanted to know what it was at its deepest core. So I pulled it towards me – towards my awareness. My desire to really know the truth about this was intense. I was crying as hard as I could cry and I wanted to know what that was. And as I pulled this deep sorrow into me, I wondered what that enormous mass would feel like when it got even closer, yet to my surprise, it simply dissolved. Yes, it dissolved and it did so rather quickly. What was left was just me, just my awareness.

The sadness dissolved in a way that made me recognize that it was dissolving back into me because that is where it had come from. It was born from my awareness and it was returning to my awareness. I instantly knew intuitively that all my emotions were like that. They all arose from my awareness, were witnessed by my awareness and then dissolved back into my awareness. In this way, I also recognized that everything that I had ever experienced arose from my awareness and then dissolved. Everything. All the sensations of the five physical senses, all my thoughts, my nighttime dreams, all my intuitive feelings and all my inner senses. Everything physical and everything spiritual.

And there was more. I intuitively knew that the awareness that was looking out of my eyes was the same awareness that looks out of your eyes. There is only One Awareness, the Divine Awareness, and as such, it is the only reality that was not created. This is the One Self that arises as all apparent selves. In this way, the One becomes the many.

As I reflected back on what had just happened, I recognized that while my body was still crying, I was not dissatisfied with being so sad. I accepted it as perfectly natural and appropriate. While there had been this human sadness for me to witness, I learned that I could hold it within the larger framework of Divine Bliss.

This is like a mother who knows how to stay centered in this Divine Bliss while holding her crying child in her loving arms. She would never push away her dear child or judge it as undesirable in any way. You can be like the combination of the two of them with this Divine Bliss holding your human sadness.

This was the gift that I received from deep sorrow. Tookie's passing gave me a new understanding. His death gave me a new life. Now I know a little more about who I really am and I know the Divine Bliss that holds all human emotions. I had heard Timothy Conway talk about this for months, but now I knew it from my own personal experience.

Perhaps you will be inspired to ponder this deeply.

Chapter 7 – The Illusion of Solidness in the Dream World

Once I was helping a friend with her computer. It was on the floor with the cover off and the hard drive was in my hand. Hard drives are not very big, about the size of two decks of playing cards, yet they are very heavy and solid. My friend was telling me about a documentary about the proof of God. She detected my lack of interest and this puzzled her since she knew I was interested in spirituality. So she asked me for my thoughts. I blurted out that I could not even prove *to myself* that I was holding that hard drive, even though it seemed as solid and real as anything could be. What I meant was that I could be dreaming and if I awoke from that dream, I would realize that the hard drive did not really exist in the way that we normally think.

That very night, I had a dream where I was standing next to a metal garage door and touching it with my hand. In real life, I knew that the owner of that garage had recently replaced the door with something completely different so I knew that this was not "real life." Instead, I knew it was an ordinary nighttime dream. In the dream, I thought, "This feels like solid metal, just as solid and real as that hard drive felt at my friend's house." I was touching the metal very carefully to make sure that the tactile sensations were indeed the same, and they were. The experiential discovery that things in a dream can feel as solid as things in ordinary life was quite remarkable to me. I wondered, "How is it that something in a dream can seem so solid?"

In the second dream that we will consider for this chapter, I was touching a parked car. As before, the metal felt as solid and real as it could be. For some reason, I knew it was a dream and I thought, "Well, since this is a dream, not only should I be able to experience the metal as if it is solid, but I should also be able to put my hand right through it."

With that thought, my hand did indeed push through the metal as if it were a ghost-like object. So here was a very vivid experience where one thing could be experienced either as solid or not solid, and my thoughts seemed to be in control of that experience even though it wouldn't work that way in our ordinary world. Very interesting.

In another dream, I was hanging from a high cliff. I felt the strain on my hands, arms and shoulders as gravity pulled strongly on the weight of my body. Could I pull myself up? No way! I wasn't even sure if I could hang on for another minute! What was I going to do? The sense of danger sent a wave of fear all over me; I was surely doomed! And yet, here I am, alive and well. I lived to tell the tale! So how did I escape? Did I become lucid and fly safely down to the valley below? Nope. I just woke up. That's all. I just woke up and it all went away.

But the important point is that waking up did not really save me from any danger. *Instead, it revealed that there never really was any danger*. Now I want to be precise with my words here. It is not correct to say that dreams aren't real, as you so often hear. It's much better to say that *dreams exist as an experience*. In other words, they exist as something that you can witness and they generate genuine emotions. And since they exist in a deceptive way, they are illusions.

Now, when it comes to nighttime dreams, you can wake up *from* the dream or you can wake up *to* the dream. When you wake up *from* the dream, it stops and you find yourself in our ordinary world. When you wake up *to* the dream, the dream continues yet you are aware that it is only a dream. You are lucidly aware that you are witnessing an illusion and that nothing in the dream can harm you. You know that you will soon wake up and the dream will simply disappear. You may or may not remember it but nonetheless, the dream itself will be gone. Now you see why I like to say that you can wake up *from* the dream or *to* the dream.

More insights come when we ponder that I could not tell the difference between what solid metal felt like in my dream and what it feels like in our ordinary physical world. Does this hint at the possibility that even our ordinary reality might be a different type of dream where everything is again revealed to exist *only as an experience?* Of course our ordinary reality has some continuity to it and it seems to offer a shared stage where many people can interact. But even so, our ordinary reality could still be a type of dream that has continuity and a shared stage.

If our ordinary reality is only *real as an experience,* just like a dream, perhaps we can both wake up *from* it, and we can also wake up *to* it. I think it is possible to wake up *from* this dream without dying. This is what happens in the formless trance state called samadhi. And I think when you wake up *to* the dream of ordinary life, you bring the full wisdom of samadhi into your daily life.

Notice what happens in an ordinary dream when you become lucid and all your fears fall away. Remarkably, this fear is replaced with joy. It is not replaced with a flat, dull attitude such as "Oh, none of this matters since this is just a dream." Instead, a delightful exuberance spontaneously arise when you recognizing that you are vibrantly alive and that you are always safe because who you truly are transcends all of the circumstances of the dream. The dream has no power over your emotional state of being and cannot impair the well-being of your true self. So you can relax into your natural emotional state of being of peace and joy.

Well, the same thing happens when you wake up *to* the "dream" of our ordinary reality. This is "the great awakening" that brings unconditional peace and joy.

The dream figure that you appear to be while dreaming is not really who you truly are in the most fundamental way, it only seems like it is while you are dreaming without being lucid. But no matter if you are lucid or not, who you truly are is never in any danger from the circumstances of the dream. The real you is always safe even though the dream figure might seem to be in danger. The dream figure that seems to be you in a fundamental way *is really just your point of view while you witness the dream*. The belief that the dream can actually be dangerous is simply a false belief.

While it is true that dreams are harmless illusions, we don't discredit them since we don't discredit any of our experiences or any of our emotions.

Read those two paragraphs twice, first with the idea that I am talking about an ordinary nighttime dream and then with the idea that I am talking about our ordinary world and that the dream figure is the person you appear to be.

Now, before we go on to the next chapter, I want to point out that when I used the word "solid," I meant "firm and stable in its shape." Since you cannot put your hand through a hard drive, I said that it was solid. Yet some people point out that there is another definition which says "not having any spaces, gaps or openings." With this definition and the modern scientific understanding that all atoms are mostly empty space, you can say that a hard drive is not solid. But that is not the definition I was using and the context of the sentences makes it clear what I was saying.

By the way, I also want to add that there is no harm in speaking as if we move our bodies around in an objective world. This is a practical way of speaking and it works just fine even if it turns out that everything is created within our awareness, just like a dream. So don't toss out this practical approach just because it doesn't use the language of a more expanded perspective. That language is just too awkward to use all the time.

Okay, on to the next chapter.

Chapter 8 – Yosemite: 75 Miles

You're out in the middle of nowhere, just traveling down an old road you found a few weeks ago. You don't really need to be anywhere in particular so it doesn't matter too much which way you go, but you would like to find a nice place to relax and enjoy. You notice an old wooden road sign that says, "Yosemite – 75 miles." The sign points towards the barren wilderness. Yosemite? The word means nothing to you. You've never heard of it. And what kind of a word is that, anyway? The sign has no more information and there is nothing to entice you to go there. Heck, maybe it's even some kind of warning. If it really were a nice spot, wouldn't lots of people already be there? Wouldn't you have already heard about it? Wouldn't the sign be much more inviting? Nevertheless, you think, "Ah, why not? You only live once. It's exciting to venture into the unknown." And with that, you head on down the road.

A few days later, you walk into Yosemite Valley. Wow! And I mean, "WOW!!" What a place! Absolutely spectacular! Waterfalls? Sure, you've seen waterfalls before – plenty of times. But nothing like this! The most magnificent waterfall you could ever imagine! And so it is with everything in the valley. Take the trees, for example. Gigantic. You didn't know trees could grow that tall. The radiant beauty of Yosemite continues to reveal itself to you day after day and you soak it all up with great joy, appreciation and gratitude.

After plenty of rest and relaxation, you decide to head on back to that other road you were on. Days later, you again pass the sign that inspired you to take a chance and explore the unknown. You decide to help inspire other people by carving a picture of a waterfall next to the word "Yosemite." There, that ought to do it. And so you move on.

Some time passes and another traveler comes upon the sign. It's a little easier for her to make the choice to explore since she knows that there will be a nice waterfall waiting for her. That is, unless there has been a drought or someone is just trying to trick her and play her for a fool. But she is not concerned about that and she ventures forth.

Her experience is of course completely unique to her, as all experiences are, and yet paradoxically, in certain ways, her experience is similar to yours since she also sees the same waterfall and so forth. When she later gets back to the sign, she decides to pin a color picture of the gorgeous valley next to your carving of the waterfall. She thinks, "There, that'll help even more. I can't do enough to encourage people to visit Yosemite. What an experience!" Notice that she can only enhance the sign, not Yosemite itself.

And so it goes for even more visitors. After a while, someone sculpts a small model of the entire valley right next to the sign and someone else posts a beautiful color video. All of this is becoming quite appealing yet none of it comes close to really capturing the true scope and beauty of Yosemite, *but that is not the goal*. The sign and all of its artistic enhancements are meant to *stimulate the adventurous spirit and give it some direction*. It is meant to motivate and guide, not to capture. It is meant to inspire exploration.

As a mystic, this is what I am most passionate about. Mystics try to inspire people to explore and discover for themselves what mystics have talked about throughout all of time. Mystics know that they will never capture the fullness of any mystical experience in words, no matter how beautiful those words might be. In fact, mystics know that they cannot capture any human experience in its entirety yet the passion to help is so strong that they joyously point to the deepest mystery of life and encourage you to dive in and explore it for yourself.

Mystics do not try to explain the mystery because they know it can never be explained. But it can be pointed to; it can be described to some extent. This is what the sign and artwork pointing to Yosemite Valley are doing. If the sign could really capture Yosemite, you wouldn't need to go to Yosemite, you could just go to the sign.

In a similar way, scientists do not explain the physical world, they only describe it. Take Newton's laws of motion as an example. These laws say that if you push something, it will move in the direction that you pushed it and they describe the path that the object will take as it moves through space and time. This is done with precise equations. But notice that this is just a description, not an explanation.

When you look at the laws of the physics, you find that they often talk about time, space, energy and matter. Yet when it comes right down to it, no scientist has ever been able to fully explain what these things actually are. They can't fully explain what time really is but they can measure it and put it in an equation. They can't fully explain what space really is but they can measure it and put it in an equation. The same is true for energy and matter. Most importantly, they cannot explain why the laws of physics are the way they are.

I point this out in order to emphasize the difference between explaining and describing, and here we see that scientists are experts at describing the world. While there is great value in that, it is not the whole story. But they don't need to explain anything. They only want a practical understanding of how the world works and this is what their scientific concepts and equations give them. They realize that the true nature of time, space, energy and matter will remain largely a mystery and this allows us all to stand in wonder and awe of the world that is all around us.

In a similar way, a mystic stands in awe of the mystery of creation. They joyfully celebrate this mystery without looking for a full explanation. And yet our ancient nondual wisdom still gives us an important and practical description of the nature of reality. This is why I like to say that this wisdom offers us just a sliver of a description rather than a full explanation of God and creation. So I hope you will be comfortable letting go of the many questions that this wisdom simply cannot address.

By the way, I would like to cover one more very important point. Mystics do not intend to prove anything in the same way that scientists prove things, yet it seems that some people expect them to do so or else they won't accept what the mystics offer. Our society is very impressed by the dramatic progress of modern science and this was achieved by combining the accurate observations of repeatable experiments with clear, logical thinking under the watchful eye of the peer review process.

Science was a strong component of my education and it works great for the usual scientific subjects *but it is very important to note that personal experience is more suited to dealing with the questions that are beyond the boundaries of science*. Accurate observations and clear thinking are still vital tools (absolutely!) yet when it comes to these deep spiritual questions, we do not focus on reproducible experiments and the peer review process.

~ ~ ~ * ~ ~ ~

Now, suppose someone is walking down the street and they smell some wonderful food. They see a restaurant and they go inside. Yep, this is the place! The aromas are exquisite. They pick up the menu and read about one mouth-watering dish after another. Finally, they make their choice ... and take a big bite, right out of the menu! Their joyous anticipation is instantly transformed into a huge disappointment. What an awful taste! Besides that, there was no nutritional value in that bite and it certainly was not very filling! They made the mistake of thinking that the description was going to provide the substance.

This point is often expressed metaphorically by the saying, "Don't eat the menu." While this of course seems obvious, I sometimes see people eat the menu and then express their strong dissatisfaction. They usually say something like, "This is all worthless," while referring to all the ideas and words that have been shared during a spiritual teaching. When you expect the *sign pointing to Yosemite* to deliver the *experience of being in Yosemite*, you will indeed be disappointed. But when you understand that the ideas and words are enthusiastically pointing metaphorically to a reality that might be revealed via a personal experience, that dissatisfaction will dissolve.

Emphasizing the importance of personal experience can make some people feel left out or worried. They might wonder, "Why haven't I had a mystical experience? Will I ever have one?" Certainly their hunger for truth is genuine and deep. Is God holding back on them? Are they not worthy? Well, you are indeed loved beyond measure. Know that the right experience will come to you when it is appropriate. This is true for all experiences. Do not merely trust in this; know it. Know it with every aspect of your being. Live every moment with that wisdom. All flowers bloom when the time is right for them.

You cannot fail at this. Something is happening to you that is well beyond the control of your personal self. Your spiritual growth – your entire life – is in the hands of God, yet this is handled in a way that makes it seem as if you are in control in a limited way at the personal level. So on a practical level, engage in your life as best you can while holding the intuitive wisdom that the divine is doing everything. This is what will remove all the worry from your life.

One of India's great holy men, Meher Baba (1894-1969), said, "First, do your best, then, don't worry, be happy." The popular hit song from 1988 by Bobby McFerrin forgot to mention the part about doing your best but it is an important aspect of this simple insight.

When it comes to your own spiritual path, it can be helpful to have a well-matched teacher who can inspire you and give you some guidance in a way that you are comfortable with. Maybe you will relax about finding a good teacher when you realize that you are only looking for something that works well for you now rather than something that is absolutely correct for everyone throughout all of time, a tall order indeed!

A mystical experience is not something that you can put into a laboratory and repeat on demand. My experience with Tookie Williams did not happen in a science lab. This is why I say that mystics do not intend to prove anything in the same way that scientists prove things. We want to inspire you to explore on your own so that you can discover the 3-D dinosaur for yourself even if society's leaders tell you that it doesn't exist. We want to inspire you to follow the sign to Yosemite. How will your adventure unfold? No one knows. How exciting!

And paradoxically, this sign metaphorically points right to where you already are, right to your pure, open awareness! But this awareness is not a thing that someone can possess, so it is much better to simply say that this sign points to the One Awareness rather than "your" awareness.

And perhaps you will enjoy this thought: Although you cannot actually point to this Awareness since it does not literally exist in space; you can flip it around and say metaphorically that space exists in the open capacity of this Awareness. Metaphorically, time, space, energy and matter are all created within this Awareness.

This is why the ancients said that you are not in the world, but instead, the world is in you!

More on that in the next chapter.

Chapter 9 – Your True Self Is the One Divine Awareness

1) Hear the truth
2) Ponder the truth
3) Meditate on the truth

These three steps cultivate the unfolding of this profound wisdom within us. They were first enunciated in the Hindu Advaita Vedanta tradition nearly 3,000 years ago. And these steps are not just completed like a checklist: one, two, three, and done. You do them in whatever order they arise and repeat them as many times as necessary. Indeed, this was very helpful for me and I continue to use all three steps.

The pondering of this truth nurtures the cognitive aspect of this wisdom while meditation nurtures its intuitive aspect. Each helps the other unfold like one hand washing the other. When I ponder this truth, I explore it from as many different angles as I can find that are fruitful. There are lots of different thoughts and ideas. When I meditate on it, I dwell on just the thought of being Source-Awareness while knowing that this has always been the truth. This chapter will help you with the first two steps and inspire you to work on the third when you put the book down.

For me, the inquiry into my True Self became a gentle yet passionate curiosity, devoid of any urgency or need. Every week, I returned to hear Timothy tell us all yet again that we were fundamentally pure, open Awareness, the Divine Source of all creation. I spent many hours in nature just thinking about being pure, open, unbounded Awareness. After about six months, I was starting to understand this not just from an intellectual point of view, but also from my direct intuitive experience. Yet it was my experience with the passing of Tookie Williams that took my understanding to a new level.

Obviously, no one can plot a path to a guaranteed mystical experience. There is no such thing as an enlightenment factory where you put regular people in one end and get enlightened people out of the other end. Yet you can do some things that might help and these three steps are like working a garden that brings forth spiritual understanding.

So clear some fertile ground and plant the seeds of genuine wonder and sincere curiosity. Water this garden everyday with contemplation and meditation and know that whatever is a perfect match for you will grow. With humility, ask yourself, "Who am I fundamentally?" By this I mean stripped of everything that is not essential to who or what you truly are. This approach will take you beyond the confines of what society tries to hold you to. While your family and friends frequently have your best interests at heart, it is often your fear of what will happen to your closest and most intimate relationships that keeps you stuck in the conventional view of who or what you seem to be.

It looks to me like most people today don't want to spend much time sincerely contemplating what they really are in the most fundamental way. They seem fairly locked into the idea that they are either just a body or both a body and a soul, and they don't think there is any reason to question those beliefs. For whatever reason, they just want to improve the conditions of their life via work, prayer, affirmations or whatever. While I certainly think it is important to work towards making the world a better place for everyone, I suggest that you at least take some time to explore what you really are in the deepest way. The rewards are priceless.

One thing that helped me was my intuitive feeling that I was more than just my body. That started when I was only about four years old. So it was very easy for me to embrace the idea of an eternal soul when I was formally taught that in Catholic school. Although I left organized religion when I was 20, this intuitive knowledge seemed to grow stronger in 1980 when I read some of the Seth books by Jane Roberts and it became even stronger in the mid-to-late 1980s when I attended many live channeling sessions.

Yet it was the satsangs with Timothy that finally gave me the guidance that I had been missing. Pondering and meditating on this timeless, open Awareness was the key to correctly understanding what I am in the most fundamental way. Do you have an intuitive knowing that you exist outside of time rather than within time? Perhaps reflecting on your true nature as timeless Awareness rather than as an eternal soul which is progressing along a spiritual path will nurture this intuitive feeling.

Let's back up a bit and contemplate the conventional scientific idea of who you are, which is a materialist view. As I touched on earlier, a materialist understands the self as the body and all the processes that arise within the body. In this view, your mind and your personal power of sentience arise from the biochemistry of your body and brain, and your personality is just the particular way that your mind functions with your unique, individualized tendencies. All your emotions arise from the combination of your thoughts, your brain activity and your biochemistry. So all of this starts with the body and continues to depend upon the body for its functionality. In this view, the physical universe is the totality of reality and the body, along with its "emergent properties," such as sentience and intelligence, make up the personal self. And in many ways, this seems very reasonable.

Yet as I pointed out before, this view does not stand up to a genuine in-depth review of the research about near-death experiences, out-of-body experiences, spirit communication and past lives. While there is no need for me to go into detail about these subjects since they are already being covered by numerous excellent authors, I still want to make a few comments.

We have many NDE reports where people witness events near their body (and elsewhere) from an out-of-body point of view. While plenty of NDEs happen without any medical attendants present, some NDEs happen when scientific instruments are monitoring the functions of the body and brain. I find these cases to be especially interesting since some experiencers later correctly reported what they saw and heard even though they did not have any vital signs at all and their eyes were closed. *Sometimes what they saw and heard was far away from their physical eyes and ears.*

In one famous case, the patient saw a single shoe on the outside ledge of the hospital building. When a disbelieving social worker assigned to the patient went to check if it was really there, she got quite a surprise. It was exactly as the patient described and not visible except from one room that was not the patient's and it was only visible if you pressed your face up against the window.

The materialists claim that a reenactment 17 years after the event proved that the shoe could have been seen in a normal way and therefore nothing paranormal happened. I find their explanation to be unconvincing since I think they placed the shoe in a different spot that was easily visible. Yet no matter what, I certainly think that there are many genuine NDEs, and also many compelling out-of-body experiences that have happened without an NDE.

These OOBEs and NDEs clearly reveal that eyes, ears and EEG brain wave activity are not required for you to see and hear the events that occur in our ordinary material world. This isn't just absolutely stunning; it means that the materialist paradigm is hopelessly flawed, and we have to throw it out the window. But what do we replace it with? What is doing the perceiving if it is not the physical body and the brain? Is it the soul? Or is it something else, something that is not even "a thing." Let's look into this.

What Is Personal Consciousness?

If you take a bite of some delicious food, you will taste it but I will not. Since I cannot directly sense your physical sensations, feel your emotions, know your thoughts, remember your memories, and so forth, it seems logical to say that we each have our own personal consciousness, separate and distinct, and this is indeed what the nondual tradition accepts as an apparent reality. Yet we need to distinguish the "layers" that combine to create this effect.

While it seems like your personal consciousness is what perceives our world, in truth, your personal consciousness has no sentience of its own; it perceives nothing. It is like a window and a window cannot see anything. Yet your personal consciousness provides a unique and dynamic point of view used by the One Awareness. Only this Awareness has the power to perceive.

What we think of as our personal power of perception is actually the sentience of the One True Self sensing the world through the point of view of our personal consciousness.

The ancient texts use the word "jiva" to refer to the personal consciousness and Timothy also translates this as "the soul" or "the viewpoint." All four terms mean the same thing. Timothy emphasizes that your personal consciousness is not a limited or smaller version of this Absolute Awareness with a diminished or restricted power of perception.

Your body also lacks any sentience yet it provides a unique viewpoint into our physical world. When you were born, the viewpoint of your soul combined with the viewpoint of your body and the two together offered a new perspective into our physical world. During normal waking consciousness, the One Awareness uses this perspective to witness all the objects and events that are within the scope of this perspective. So Awareness, body and soul work together.

*What was created when you were born was not a new
sentient being, but a new perspective from which the One
True Self perceives the world. This has been happening ever
since you were born and it is happening right now. What is
commonly thought of as your own personal sentience is really
the One Divine Awareness looking out through your own eyes!*

By the way, this is why the Buddha gave us the wonderfully
paradoxical Vajracchedika (Diamond Cutter) Sutra: "One
must save all sentient beings" [and] "there are no sentient
beings." Of course there are beings, and these beings do
appear to be sentient. But they are not really what is
sentient. Only the One Awareness is sentient.

Imagine you are the One Awareness and that you are in
a room with many windows. When you look out into the
world through one of these windows, you see a certain view.
In this way, you have all the experiences of one particular
person. You see what they see, feel what they feel, think
what they think, remember what they remember, dream
what they dream and so forth. When you look through a
different window, you have all the experiences of another
person. But you are still the same Awareness; this has not
changed in any way.

If you experienced all of these perceptions altogether
through one big window, it would be just a huge jumble
of color, noise and so forth. Our individuated personal
consciousnesses or windows are what allow the One
Awareness to have all the experiences of billions of different
people without it being one big, messy overlay. This is how
the One becomes the many.

Note that drugs and alcohol affect the body and the brain
but not the Awareness. If someone is drunk, this window
becomes unclear or distorted but the Awareness still has
perfect 20/20 vision, so to speak. So while this Awareness is
not affected at all, the overall experience is much different.

Although your personal consciousness (your soul) does not vitally depend upon your body, it uses the body to create that razor sharp feeling of being present in our physical world as a human being with a physical body. It feels like your body is an integral part of you because your personal consciousness permeates your body. Imagine a driver not only getting into a car but also infusing himself or herself into every single atom of the car. When you add to this the One Awareness looking out through the combined viewpoint of the body and soul, you get the extremely vivid experience that tricks you into falsely believing that you are a separate, mortal, sentient, physical being. You certainly do not appear to be divine in any way.

While many people have heard that the world is an illusion, few people have heard that they also are an illusion. But please don't misunderstand me. This "personal self" is most certainly real as an extremely vivid ongoing experience, but this is a deceptive reality, an illusion. You are being tricked into believing the false idea that you are fundamentally a separate, mortal, sentient, physical being rather than this pure Divine Awareness. Since all good illusions are persistent, under normal states of consciousness, it will always seem as if you are fundamentally this "sentient being." But now you will know that this is just a misleading experience, an illusion. This "personal self" is your functional identity rather than your fundamental identity.

Your personal consciousness associates with your body and it is this association that can be temporarily released during an out-of-body experience. At that time, it associates with your subtle body and a similar thing happens during a dream when it associates with your dream body.

There is a metaphor about people being hand puppets through which the True Self expresses itself and experiences the world. How good is this metaphor? Well, I think it's pretty good but it might leave you puzzled since you know without a doubt that you are not a hand puppet. You know that when you choose to pick up a pencil, it feels like it is you who evaluates your choices, decides what you want to do, and then initiates and completes the action. Picking up the pencil does not feel like it is outside of your control. There is no sensation of your arm being controlled by a different entity, a higher force, or a higher mind. You never feel like shouting out, "Hey, leave me alone and let me do my own thing!"

Well, it feels like you move your arm because you, as the True Self, do move it. The True Self moves everything while your personal self moves nothing. But since you cannot see the formless True Self and you can only see your body, it seems like you are the body-mind and that your body-mind is autonomous.

Ah, but in reality, you are the puppet master and you have mistaken the puppet as you. The puppet master and the puppet are blended together so closely that the puppet master is looking right through the eyes of the puppet. Your personal "self" is the powerless puppet while your True Self is the grand puppet master, the One Self that arises as all apparent "selves." The person is an inert yet dynamically animated puppet but you are not the puppet; you are not the person in a fundamental way.

By the way, recognizing that you are not fundamentally the person does not stop the sense or experience that makes it seem like you are, just like the recognition that the sun does not go around the earth does not stop the experience that makes it seem like it does. The sense that you are the person may lessen in its intensity, and it may seem more like you are witnessing the events of "your" life rather than having them happen to "you" the person. But this sense of being the person is really there to provide some functionality so it won't disappear completely except in deep dreamless sleep and in the formless trance state of samadhi.

Just as your personal consciousness provides a unique but limited perspective that the One Unlimited Awareness uses to perceive the world, your body provides a unique but limited puppet that the One Unlimited Power animates within the world. The puppet is limited but the Power is not.

So your personal self is not really a "self" in the true sense of the word since it is not your fundamental identity. It is also not autonomous. It is not the source of what appears to be its own will or power. It is not the source of what appears to be its own sentience.

As I touched on in Chapter 2, this reminds me of the light from the moon. It looks as if the moon is the source of its own light, but in reality, the moon is not the original source of any light at all. The source of this "moonlight" is of course, the sun. When this light comes to us directly from the sun, we call it sunlight but if it reflects off the moon, we then call it moonlight. So moonlight is really sunlight even though we make a distinction between the two.

Now image that we had lots of moons in the sky. They would each appear to be a separate source of their own light and yet the truth would be that the sun would be the only source of all that light. So it is with your "personal sentience." It appears as if each person is the unique source of their own sentience and yet there really is only One Awareness looking through each and every personal consciousness.

Similarly, what appears to be your "personal mind," your "personal will" and your "personal power" are truly the One Mind, the One Will and the One Power working through the apparent self, the person.

The One Awareness is fully aware of everything in the cosmos yet the personal self only seems to be aware of its own ever-changing experience. The One Self is sensing everyone's sensations yet the personal self appears to be sensing only its own sensations. The One Mind is thinking everyone's thoughts yet the personal self appears to be thinking only its own thoughts. Similar things can be said about the One Will and the One Power. In this way, God creates within the personal consciousness the sense that "this is me." But this limited experience of the personal self only exists as an apparent ongoing experience in our world of form, in this spectacular "play of consciousness."

Some people talk about a regular self (the body-mind) and a higher self (the soul), and in a way, this can be helpful since together they make up the person that we call "me." And I will continue to use phrases like "personal self," "functional self" or "apparent self" in my writings and conversations to refer to the person. But the deepest truth is that you only have one True Self, this Source-Awareness. Yet even so, these other phrases can still be quite useful.

More About the Play, the Actor and the Character

In the first chapter, I touched on the metaphor of an actor arising as a character in a play. Let's go further with this metaphor right now.

Our ordinary reality is the larger framework that holds the fabricated story of the play. Since the play has its own framework, we see that the bigger framework holds the smaller one. You might say that the play is one level down. The bigger framework transcends the smaller one. Within the context of our ordinary world, the play is *real as a play*, even though the story it tells is fictional. It exists as a fictional construction. So in a funny way you can say that the play is real as a fictional story.

Everyone sees that the characters and events of the play are only valid and meaningful within the context of the play, and that within the context of our ordinary reality, they exist only as fiction. We all clearly understand that with the play there is a layer of pretending. The real police will not show up and arrest the actor who plays a murderer because the actor is only pretending and no one was really murdered. This pretending is what allows us to safely create and enjoy all kinds of dramas and stories which can generate real emotions within us. Even though the stories are fictional, our emotions are real.

In order for the play to work, the audience must overlook the actor and completely accept the character. Now suppose the actor becomes so totally absorbed in his role that he too completely overlooks who he really is and instead, just thinks that he is only the character. This is similar to what we have in our world. The One Invisible Actor is playing all the roles yet "overlooking" its formless nature. In this way, it is hiding from itself and pretending to forget what is really going on. But you cannot really hide yourself from yourself and you will not pretend to forget forever.

Our ordinary reality is like a play that is fabricated within the greater framework of Source-Awareness. The people and events are valid and meaningful only within the context of this constructed fictional story we call ordinary reality.

The One True Self arises as each and every person just like an actor arises as a character. The One True Self creates all the personal selves, permeates them, animates them, and transcends them. It uses them all as instruments and as viewpoints. This paradoxical combination of permeation and transcendence is why we say that the One True Self is in the world but not of it.

Let's go a little further with this metaphor. Let's suppose that in the play there is a house on fire and there is a person trapped in the house. The character is a fireman who obviously is supposed to go in and save the person. Can the character push back and say to the actor, "Whoa! That looks really dangerous! I'm not going in there! I mean, you can go in there if you want, but I'm not going. In fact, I saw a much more romantic scene over on another stage. That's where I'm going. You can do what you want"? No, of course not. The character has no will or power of its own; it is a perfect conduit for the actor's wishes. Even if the actor wanted to share his will and power with the character in a 50-50 split, that couldn't happen since the character is completely inert. The actor and the character do not co-create the fireman's role in the play. It is completely created by the actor.

I had only recently started to attend Timothy's satsangs when he just matter-of-factly stated, "There is no co-creation." I thought, "Boy, he isn't shy about tossing that idea right out the window." But once you see that God is doing everything, well, you just tell it like you see it. No fanfare is needed.

Furthermore, notice that the actor must always be himself. There is no way to change that. Of course the actor can start and stop this extra mode of being the character at any time but even still, he is always the actor. This is why I like to say the following:

The Infinite comes forth in ways that make it appear finite. The Immortal comes forth in ways that make it appear mortal. The Divine comes forth in ways that make it appear to be only human. But our Infinite Reality is only appearing to be limited. That which is Awakeness itself is only appearing to be something that can be asleep. That which is Aliveness itself is only appearing to be something that can die. The only Reality that is present is this divine Source-Awareness.

Source-Awareness is unchanging since there are no qualities or aspects that could change. Source-Awareness exists as this unchanging capacity to create and this unchanging capacity to perceive. This is what creates and witnesses all ever-changing phenomena. This is what arises as all worlds and all objects within those worlds. This is the One Self that arises as all personal consciousnesses within those worlds.

Source-Awareness cannot become happy or sad in a fundamental way yet it can animate an inert puppet in a way that exhibits the characteristics of happiness and sadness. These characteristics are witnessed by the True Self while the personal self witnesses and experiences nothing. It is not sentient. It is not alive.

This fabulous Awareness – your True Self – creates the experience of what seems like a separate individual person living his or her own life. This is such a delightful paradox. You are one-hundred percent Divine and simultaneously, you arise as a person that is one-hundred percent human. Through the mystery of creation, the One seems to come forth as the many. Magnificent!

Absolute Awareness, Universal Consciousness and Personal Consciousness

Now is a good time to talk about universal consciousness, which is sometimes called the primordial seed-vibration or the creative manifesting principle. This is the first vibration through which all other vibrations come. It is distinct from Absolute Awareness, which is the vibrationless witness and ultimate Source of all vibrations.

Timothy offers us this:

> The most ancient Upanishad wisdom texts speak of "Brahman" (Absolute Reality) and the "pranava" (AUM/ OM, the primordial seed-vibration for the multi-level cosmos). This is also referred to as Brahman and Maya, the illusory play of the Absolute, which is "relatively real, experientially vivid, but ultimately dreamlike." This is why the sages of ancient India differentiated the

unchanging, formless, silent Absolute Awareness (the "Noumenon") from the "universal consciousness," which is always changing and constantly morphing, with its dynamic vibrational forms arising as the ever-changing play of phenomena.

In later Hindu tradition, the eminent sage Shankara (who codified in his commentaries and treatises so much of the wisdom of the Upanishads) distinguished this as "Nirguna Brahman" (formless, "qualityless" Reality) and "Saguna Brahman" (Reality with form, qualities, and dynamism). The Hindu Bhakti and then Tantra traditions distinguished this as "Shiva" and "Shakti."

The Buddhists and Daoists have their own way of distinguishing the formless, unchanging, unborn Absolute from the Absolute-playing-as-phenomena.

So do the Christians: God (or the "Godhead") and the Logos/"Word," the primordial Divine vibration by which the One Divine God creates/emanates the "many creatures."

In Islam and Sufism, this is "Allah" and "Allah's veil of creation."

In Daoism, this is the "Dao" and its power, "De." An old formulation runs: "From the Dao (the Absolute) comes the 'one' (the principle of manifestation), from the one comes the 'two' (yin and yang), from the two come the five (the Chinese 5-element schema) and from the five come the 'ten thousand things.'"

The reason why it is so important to have this distinction between Absolute Awareness and universal consciousness (the creative manifesting principle) is that the products or cosmic manifestations of the universal consciousness experientially disappear [from the experience of a person] in deep dreamless sleep and the formless trance state of nirvikalpa samadhi, hence they cannot be the Absolute. The deeper continuity of Supreme Identity IS and ALWAYS IS, regardless of whether a world of phenomena is arising or not.

The great sages knew by pure, Divine intuition that underlying all that is changeable is THIS CHANGELESS CONTINUITY OF IDENTITY, the true "I AM," unconditional BEING. Whereas by contrast everything else is changeable, passing, coming in and out of existence. This includes the sense of a manifest cosmos, even on just a very, very subtle, psychic/heavenly level.

Timothy points out that his mentor Sri Nisargadatta, whom he visited shortly before he passed away in 1981, and Ramana Maharshi, who passed away in1950, were two sages of the modern era who understood the distinction between Absolute Awareness (Shiva), universal consciousness (Shakti) and personal consciousness (jiva). While several other modern sages wrote about this with some clarity, most did not make a distinction between universal consciousness and Absolute Awareness, probably because they were still tied to the subtlest level of phenomena, which is universal consciousness.

Transcendent Absolute Awareness emanates as the objects of Awareness, which are known through an ever-changing experience. When I asked Timothy if there really was an objective outside world, he just replied that this question did not lead to liberation. And with that clarification, I finally let go of my desire to find a definitive answer to that burning question. And again, as I mentioned in an earlier chapter, it is perfectly fine to speak as if we move our bodies around in an objective world. Speaking from the absolute perspective is just too awkward and most people would not understand us anyway. So who needs that, right?

Please note that your personal consciousness does not create the objects that fall within its scope. Everything is created by the dynamic power of universal consciousness which is sourced in Absolute Awareness, your True Self. When someone walks into a room, *their experience* of that room is created in that moment, but the room was already there. The room will not disappear when everyone in it leaves. You can prove this by making a video recording of it. Each person is dynamically moved through space and time by the One Self and this allows Absolute Awareness to witness and experience all that is within the scope of each personal consciousness.

During both deep dreamless sleep and nirvikalpa samadhi, all personal experiences stop while the body continues to function with regards to heartbeat, breath and cell repair. During this time, the role of the personal consciousness is shifted into a reduced or suspended mode. Even though the body lacks sensory input from the outside world to a very large extent, it still can be brought back to normal waking consciousness with sounds, lights, or a shake.

Of course during this time, the world is still available for everyone else. One person going into a formless trance state does not obliterate the entire multi-level cosmos for everyone else.

Just as OOBEs can help people shift into understanding themselves as a soul, nirvikalpa samadhi can shift people into understanding themselves as pure awareness. Going into this state is what I call waking up *from* the dream of ordinary reality since the dream goes away. Obviously, in this formless trance state, there is no functionality at all.

It is important to note that there is another type of samadhi, sahaja samadhi, which offers the full wisdom of nirvikalpa samadhi while being fully functional in the world. Moving into sahaja samadhi is what I call waking up *to* the dream of ordinary reality since the dream continues, much like a lucid nighttime dream continues. You know you are witnessing an illusion. All fear falls away. You know that what you witness in our world cannot affect your True Self and the recognition of this truth is what liberates the personal consciousness. Now you see why I like to say that you can wake up *from* the dream and you can wake up *to* the dream of our ordinary world.

Now, we say that creation is relatively real for two reasons. The first is that creation is only known through experience, which requires the relative relationship of the observer and the objects which are observed. But creation is also literally dependent upon Source-Awareness for its very existence and substance. This is it's vital relationship.

Source-Awareness exits as this unchanging capacity to perceive. It exists before time and outside of space as the unchanging Source of time, space and everything else. This is why Source-Awareness is said to be Absolutely Real.

Who you are as Awareness is completely imperceptible so you cannot get to know yourself by observing yourself. Yet your own existence as Source-Awareness gives birth to the intuitive wisdom that you exist as pure Source-Awareness. This intuitive wisdom is placed into the consciousness of the person where you can witness it. The ancient texts call this wisdom *"knowing by being."*

Again, our lives exists for us as an extremely vivid experience. This is why it is so easy to believe that our fundamental identity is the body-mind and that there really is a solid world outside of that. Timothy offers this about why there is this vividness:

> It's because you are Awareness playing as the power
> of consciousness that everything feels so vivid. [...] It's
> because of consciousness, not because of atoms, or

molecules, or cells, or clusters of cells, organs and
tissues. That's not why there's a vividness [...]. It's
because you, the personal consciousness [jiva], through
the power of primordial consciousness [Shakti], rooted
in Absolute Awareness [Shiva], animate all of this,
enliven it, spark it up, fire it with the living flame of love.

Only Absolute Awareness Is Alive Under Its Own Power

Our ancient texts tell us that all of creation is inert ("jada").
Yet animals, plants and other lifeforms are spontaneously
animated by the Unseen Power in a way that makes them
appear to be alive, according to our conventional definition
of life. On a practical level, it makes perfect sense to keep our
conventional definition of life since that definition works so
well in our common conversations. It would be foolish to
throw that away.

While the conventional definition of life is certainly useful,
it is also possible to use a different definition. Our nondual
wisdom offers the view that only Absolute Awareness is
alive under its own power. This is why I often say that this
Awareness is Aliveness itself. Since Awareness fully
permeates every aspect of creation, all of creation is fully
saturated with this unbounded Aliveness.

It is with this understanding that it can be said that
everything is alive. Yet it is important to point out that
creation is not the source of its own aliveness and this is
why the ancient texts say that all of creation is inert. With
this in mind, let's go a little deeper into this idea that
everything as alive.

Imagine a person who is both deaf and blind. Even though
their physical senses are dramatically reduced, they still
know without a doubt that they exist. They have a sense
of aliveness.

Is it possible that objects, which appear to lack all of our physical senses, not just hearing and vision, still somehow have a sense of aliveness? For example, could an electron have a sense of aliveness? Just as a person has a personal consciousness, could an electron have an electron consciousness? And could a similar thing be said about everything?

Seth tells us in the Preface of his book, *The Nature of Personal Reality*:

> *All consciousness has within it the deep abiding impetus to use its abilities fully, to expand its capacities, to venture joyfully beyond the seeming barriers of its own experience. The very consciousnesses within the smallest molecules cry out against any ideas of limitation. They yearn toward new forms and experiences. Even atoms, then, constantly seek to join in new organizations of structure and meaning. They do this "instinctively."*

Later, near the end of the first chapter, he adds this:

> *Trees and rocks possess their own consciousness, and also share a gestalt consciousness [...]. The cells and organs [of your body] have their own awarenesses, and a gestalt one. So the race of man also has individual consciousness[es] and a gestalt or mass consciousness, of which you individually are hardly aware. The mass race consciousness, in its terms, possesses an identity. You are a portion of that identity while still being unique, individual and independent. You are confined only to the extent that you have chosen physical reality, and so placed yourself within its context of experience. While physical, you follow physical laws, or assumptions. These form the framework for corporeal expression.*

I find all these different types of consciousnesses quite fascinating. Although Seth did not say this exactly, it makes perfect sense to me that the mass consciousness of dogs, for example, is the source of their instinctive behavior and this is why they all behave roughly the same. Perhaps it is also true that each breed has its own mass consciousness within the bigger mass consciousness of all dogs. And yet each dog has its own individuated personal dog consciousness, which holds its own unique understanding of the world and itself, and this is why each dog behaves according to its own personality. Each individuated personal dog consciousness (dog soul) is associated with a specific dog body. The body is connected to the soul, the soul is connected to the mass consciousness and ultimately it all flows from universal consciousness and Absolute Source-Awareness.

Each personal and mass consciousness can be said to have a vibrational pattern. Because of this, we can talk about higher consciousness, lower consciousness and the refinement of consciousness. Your personal consciousness (your soul) holds beliefs about your personal self, the world, and how you fit into the world. As this understanding is purified, the vibrational pattern shifts upward.

This purification comes about through the removal of false ideas, the integration of true ideas, and the release of fear and any selfish or self-centered tendencies. God is purifying the personal consciousness and using it as an instrument in order to bring forth divine virtues. So don't worry about making a mistake. Just let go and let God purify and polish your soul. I'll say more about that in another chapter.

By the way, I think it is perfectly fine for Seth to speak from the perspective of how this appears rather than from the absolute perspective of what is really happening. So it is fine to say that "they do this 'instinctively'" instead of saying that the hand of God controls them in a way that makes it look like they are behaving instinctively all on their own. He also uses the word "awarenesses" where I would use the word "consciousnesses," but we still understand what he means.

So let's all celebrate the One Aliveness that permeates all form, some of it in a way that makes it seem alive (animals and so forth) and some of it without that quality (rocks and so forth). I find all this to be profoundly beautiful and quite amazing.

In Form, We Are Many; In Essence, We Are One

We have all heard it said, "We are all one." While I certainly think this is true, many people find this statement to be quite puzzling so let's dig into this subject a little bit further.

Some people intuitively know that we are all one. I want to be very precise here. They have the experience of perceiving an intuitive knowing that we are all this One Awareness. Obviously I think this is fantastic, yet I want to point out that they are not *directly perceiving* the One Awareness in which we are all one since the One Awareness has no aspects that can be perceived or experienced in any way whatsoever.

This Awareness has the capacity to perceive, yet it cannot be perceived.

While this intuitive knowing of oneness reveals the truth, people often try to validate it by finding pure oneness in the world of form, but this is impossible. They usually point to ways in which we are all alike or ways in which we are all connected and they offer this as examples of how we are all one. While these things can of course be used as symbols that point to the One Awareness, you cannot perceive pure oneness in form. In form, you can find closeness, intimacy, compassion, empathy, connection and so forth. Yet your body and my body are different and the same can be said about our minds, our personalities and our souls.

This is why I say that in form, we are many. But of course, fundamentally, we are One as this invisible and indivisible Divine Awareness. So instead of just saying, "We are all one," I like to say:

"In form, we are many; in essence, we are One."

This is one of the most important sentences in this book. I could also say, "In form we are unique human beings; in essence we are the One Divine Awareness." An important point is that the form is also fully divine. Don't think that only the essence is divine. Remember, ice doesn't just come *from* the water; it *is* the water. God arises as creation without dropping God's divine nature.

Max Planck's Famous Quotation

If I could, I would put the One Awareness on a table in front of everyone and announce, "That's what I'm talkin' about!" But this cannot be done since it is not an object that can be perceived. Physicist Max Planck said something like this back in 1931: "I regard consciousness as fundamental. I regard matter as a derivative from consciousness. We cannot get behind consciousness. Everything that we talk about, everything that we regard as existing, postulates consciousness."

This is similar to the view of a mystic. While Planck simply puts consciousness first with matter arising out of that consciousness, our nondual wisdom puts the One Source-Awareness first and then downstream from that, we have the one universal consciousness, plus all the objects within universal consciousness, plus all the billions of personal consciousnesses that each offer a viewpoint utilized by Source-Awareness. The distinction between consciousness and Awareness is crucial and yet it is seldom made.

Both mainstream science and Max Planck regard awareness and consciousness as the same thing, but they hold opposite views as to whether consciousness arises from the body and brain or whether it is the other way around. While I think these comments from Planck are helpful to some extent, we should note that mainstream science did not embraced them, although the core of Planck's work was accepted.

I think what Planck was getting at when he stated, "We cannot get behind consciousness," is that you cannot put the power of sentience (Awareness) on a table in front of you and then stand behind it and observe it and study it, just like scientists do when they study all other phenomena. And notice that you cannot put personal consciousness on the table in front of you either. You can only observe the objects that show up in the scope of your personal consciousness.

Max Planck is one of the founding fathers of quantum physics and with this statement, he is not claiming that physics has explained human consciousness. Nor is he saying that human consciousness is formally discussed in the theory of quantum physics. (Some people mistakenly think that consciousness plays a role in the double slit experiment but what is really involved is a device called a detector, which "observes" what happens.) Instead, Planck is just saying that consciousness lies outside the scope of what object-oriented science can study, and stating his belief that consciousness is more fundamental than any object.

Scientists study "consciousness" by studying the body and brain during different states such as our normal waking state, the sleep state, the meditative state and so forth. But they are not really studying personal consciousness or pure Awareness. They are just studying the body and brain.

Science is the fruit of observation, logic and the peer review process. Our nondual wisdom is the fruit of observation, logic, personal experience and intuition.

By the way, Timothy makes a distinction between spiritual intuition and psychic intuition. To tune into the spiritual energies that are about to show up in the physical world is to tune into psychic intuition. To tune into spiritual truth as revealed by the One Divine Mind is to tune into spiritual intuition. One is focused on spiritual phenomena; the other is focused on spiritual truth. Timothy suggests that we not place any special focus on psychic intuition and instead, open ourselves to spiritual intuition. The steps that take you to the understanding of yourself as pure awareness and then to the understanding that this is the One Source-Awareness, the Self of all selves, comes via spiritual intuition so you can see why it can be helpful to be open to its gifts.

Firsthand and Secondhand Modes of Knowing Truth

For you to abide in the full flow of all available wisdom, it is helpful to have all modes of discovering truth open and working together in harmony. This includes direct observation of things and events (inner and outer), rational thought, and also intuitive revelation. These are all firsthand modes of knowing truth and to this we should also add secondhand knowledge that comes to us from the work of others.

For example, if you want to understand how physics works, you should get a good book or a good teacher or both. If a chemist tells you that mixing two chemicals together is a bad idea, you should heed this advice because this is his or her area of expertise. So when it comes to subjects that you are not knowledgeable about, it makes perfect sense to consult an expert in the field and this is why secondhand knowledge has its place. But be on the lookout for both innocent mistakes and intentional deception since no one's perfect and not all "experts" have our best interest at heart.

Since I have never had a near-death experience, I chose to learn about them from books written by people who have had them. I also read books about out-of-body experiences, spirit communication and past lives. While books on these four subjects do provide an interesting perspective, they only offer secondhand knowledge to me, not the firsthand knowledge that I prefer. Yet this is still valuable.

And it is worth noting that almost all the books about OOBEs do include a guide on how you can try to develop this skill yourself, if you are so inclined.

Incidentally, I have noticed that many people who have had an NDE or an OOBE are stuck at the point of understanding themselves as a soul or an autonomous spiritual entity. Of course it is great to move beyond the materialist point of view, but there is still the deeper wisdom which offers us the idea that your fundamental identity is this formless Source-Awareness.

Obviously, this nondual wisdom does not come alive within you with tremendous vitality when it is only secondhand news. This is why Timothy doesn't ask us to simply believe what he says about this ancient wisdom. But hearing the truth is only the first step of the three steps that we saw at the beginning of this chapter and Timothy encourages us to "check it out for yourself," which is done via the other two steps. He often asks, "What is it that is closer than the mind? What is it that is aware of the content of the mind?" The answer seems to be your own awareness, yet this turns out to be the One Divine Awareness.

It has become popular to talk about "being present." This state, which is also known as Buddhist mindfulness, Hindu witnessing, and Sufi and Christian watchfulness, pays close attention to some of the objects that are within the scope of your personal consciousness. While this does indeed provide a richer experience of the moment, the main benefit comes when it brings about the awakening that you are this unchanging awareness that witnesses all these ever-changing things. This wisdom will eventually grow into the full understanding that this awareness is Source-Awareness, that which creates everything and depends on nothing.

While this state of mindfulness can lead to this wisdom, there is no need to become obsessed with it. Use it whenever you wish but allow yourself the freedom to experience any and all states. Notice that a more functional state is required to get through your daily activities, so it is not desirable or even possible to be locked into perpetual mindfulness.

Even though mystics present a view about your own true nature that conflicts with the common views presented by society and religion, you do not have to worry about whom to believe since you can look into this for yourself. And a mystic may inspire you to ponder some things that you might otherwise overlook.

Everyone knows that they are aware but most people make the "mistake" of carrying this too far and they incorrectly conclude that they are a being that is aware rather than simply pure awareness itself. We are so used to thinking that in order for seeing to take place, there must be a physical (or spiritual) being that sees. Yet the truth is that there is seeing but there is no object-like being that sees and this is why it is sometimes said that there is no seer, although I prefer the way this is presented in the Brhadaranyaka Upanishad. It tells us that this One Awareness is "the unseen seer of seeing, the unheard hearer of hearing, the unfelt feeler of feelings" and it goes on. This Awareness is the unsensed sensor of all phenomena and to this I like to add that this Source-Awareness is also the undreamt dreamer of dreams.

We have all heard it said that you are not a human being having a spiritual experience, but instead, you are a spiritual being having a human experience. While that shift in understanding is of course very important, there is still a

78

deeper wisdom. In truth, you are not a being of any kind, physical or spiritual. You are pure awareness! And most importantly, this awareness is the Divine Awareness, the only reality that was not created. This Divine Awareness is the Source of all of creation and it is the only witness to it. This is your true fundamental self and it is looking out of your eyes right now!

How Is This True?

Someone once repeated for me the ancient teaching, "There is no doer." Since my understanding at that time was that everyone was busy doing lots of things, this seemed to me to be complete nonsense, but I decided to cast off my conflicting understanding and approach the statement from the perspective of asking "How is this true?" The normal scientific approach is to examine a statement by looking for a way to demonstrate that it is false. If nothing can be found to counter it, then it is accepted as true and this works great for all the subjects that science is good at. But when it comes to spiritual understandings, there can be fruit in this other approach.

This is what helped me realize that this invisible Power does everything. So there is a doer, but it has no thing-like qualities. There is doing, but there is no thing or being that does anything. Everything that the personal self seems to do is done by this invisible animating Power. This is one of the central teachings of the most ancient Chinese Daoists and more recently highlighted by the great Indian sage Nisargadatta, and it is a key teaching presented at our weekly satsang gatherings.

So when you ponder some of these puzzling spiritual principles, try the approach of asking "How is this true?" Perhaps you will have some breakthroughs like I did.

What Is Enlightenment?

Although there is no universally accepted definition of enlightenment, here are the two key criteria that I use:

1) *Being fully awake* to the intuitive understanding of your True Self as this One Divine Source-Awareness, the One Self that arises as all apparent selves and

2) *Being completely free* from all selfish or self-centered desires and tendencies, which are sometimes called egocentric binding likes and dislikes.

These two aspects work together to automatically produce the unhindered flow of all the divine virtues such as loving kindness, compassion, joy, peaceful equanimity, humility, generosity, and patience. This is the fruit of enlightenment, which is treasure you hold on the inside. Unlike the treasure you hold on the outside, you *can* take this with you.

The first aspect of enlightenment seems to unfold somewhat suddenly, usually through a series of awakening experiences, while the second aspect unfolds slowly through gradual cultivation over many lifetimes. This was noted long ago in the Chan (Chinese), Seon (Korean) and Zen (Japanese) traditions. Both aspects unfold at the same time, it's just that the first aspect seems to have some stairsteps while the second aspect is more like a ramp.

No single awakening experience will immediately produce the completely finished liberation spoken of in the second aspect, yet all of these awakenings together will eventually lead to full liberation. In time, all selfish and self-centered desires and tendencies will soften and be washed away.

When you are free from selfish desires and tendencies, you will be open to everything that arises while being kind and compassionate towards everyone. In this regard, Timothy often points out that being open to the flow of life does not mean you should just sit back and accept everything that happens without doing anything to make things better, especially when it comes to injustice.

Just because God is doing everything, including acts that we commonly call evil, does not mean that we should give up our common sense when it comes to trying our best to make the world a better place. If you are working for justice, do so in a wholesome way without directing any anger or hatred towards the people who are behaving in a harmful way. If people have to be put in jail, do so for rehabilitation rather than punishment and in a way that is respectful.

While this chapter focuses on the first aspect of enlightenment, the next two chapters will go into more detail on the second aspect.

Although these awakenings seem to happen suddenly, they are never instantly complete, just like waking up in the morning. These awakenings always have a period of deepening, and this deepening can last years or even lifetimes. During this time, these concepts are transformed from mere ideas into a living truth that burns within your soul.

While there are many spiritual awakenings, here I want to talk about three specific awakenings that pertain to "your" awareness. These awakenings can occur in any order or in any combination, including all at once. So in my writing here, when I say first, second and third, I am only referring to their order in this presentation, and not necessarily the order that they will occur for you.

The first awakening is the one that I've already touched on many times: "Ah, I am not *fundamentally* my body, and I am not even *fundamentally* my soul. Instead, *I am fundamentally pure awareness!*"

The second awakening is this: "Ah, the awareness that's looking out of my eyes is the same awareness that's looking out of your eyes ... and his eyes ... and her eyes ... and the eyes of every sentient being on all the worlds, both physical and spiritual. There is only one Awareness."

Now, when I use this phrase "one awareness," it's not because you can see it and count it, because as I mentioned earlier, this awareness is completely imperceptible in every way. So instead, we use this phrase "one awareness," to emphasize the idea of wholeness. This awareness never breaks itself into pieces, whether those pieces are disconnected or connected. No, this awareness never breaks itself into pieces at all.

Furthermore, this awareness is not like a tree with a trunk of the one awareness that grows into a branch of your awareness, and into a different branch of his awareness, and into a different branch of her awareness and so forth. No, this awareness never branches out at all. This awareness is always whole.

There is only one Awareness. That's the second awakening.

The third awakening is this: *This awareness arises as each and every thing that it is aware of.*

What we are talking about here is God and creation – Awareness (God) and the objects of awareness (creation). It is very simple.

When I use this phrase "objects of awareness," I am talking about anything at all that can be perceived in any way at all. So I am not just talking about physical objects, I am also talking about thoughts, emotions, nighttime dreams, intuitive feelings, energy states, hallucinations, and so forth. Anything at all that can be perceived in any way at all is an object of awareness.

Now, with this particular awakening, we recognize the second capacity of this awareness. This Awareness has both *the capacity to perceive* and *the capacity to create what it perceives*. This process of creation is best described as an emanation – a spontaneous emanation – and this Awareness is the source of this emanation. Because of this, Timothy and I refer to this Awareness as "Source-Awareness."

This Source-Awareness emanates as the totality of created reality and this Source-Awareness is what you truly are fundamental. And, as you have heard me say before, this Source-Awareness is looking out of your eyes right now! *Not a piece of it. Not a branch of it. The wholeness of this Source-Awareness is looking out of your eyes right now!*

More About Enlightenment

Earlier I said that there is no such thing as an enlightenment factory where you put regular people in one end and get enlightened people out of the other end. But in a way, there is. All of creation is this enlightenment factory since everything is unfolding via the will of God and in this way, God is revealing God to God. Everything is unfolding with perfect timing so you are always on time no matter what. All your spiritual revelations will happen for you at the exact right time and therefore you do not have to concern yourself with this in any special way. Just live your life and follow your bliss in a wholesome, unselfish way with unconditional love for everyone and without fear of what will unfold.

We have all heard it said that before enlightenment, we have to chop wood and carry water, and that after enlightenment, we still have to chop wood and carry water. I'm not sure that a modern marketing department would want to stress this point since it makes it sound like there's no practical benefit to enlightenment. But there really are profoundly practical benefits which grow daily as this understanding becomes clearer. While your daily tasks and problems won't go away, your worry about them will gradually dissolve completely. With this, your problems are transformed into just things to work on. Without worry, you are free to abide continuously in Divine Bliss while chopping wood and carrying water.

This is how this ancient nondual wisdom becomes oh so very practical! Love, joy and peace cascade from within, flowing freely into your experience without any hindrance, always unconditional available.

An ancient text talks about how God is making a flute out of us. Slowly but surely, with the skill of a master craftsman, the flute is being hollowed out and tuned to perfection. Of course the flute will not play itself, but thankfully, God will use it to play delightfully divine music.

Now, let's clear up a few misunderstandings about what might indicate that someone is enlightenment.

Some people have spiritual powers called siddhis. There are quite a few siddhis including knowing the minds of others, the ability to manifest things out of thin air, the perfect accomplishment of one's will, and more. But just because someone has some of these powers does not mean that they are fully enlightened. They could be devoid of compassion, caught up in self-aggrandizement, and just using these powers for selfish gains. But let's hope not.

Another common belief is that people who can go into samadhi are enlightened or close to it. Although the ability to enter the formless trance state of nirvikalpa samadhi does not mean that this person is enlightened, an enlightened person does have this ability. So this is necessary but not sufficient. This trance state does not immediately bring full awakening nor does it instantly purify the personal consciousness by removing all selfish and self-centered desires and tendencies.

Timothy suggests that you not chase after samadhi or any other special state and instead recognize that your True Self is the source and substance of all such states. Occasionally exploring formless samadhi will show that the personal consciousness is not supreme. It is not your True Self.

I should also mention that kundalini experiences often indicate spiritual growth but do not prove enlightenment.

You cannot obtain enlightenment by your own doing. It is something that comes to you from God at a time when the Divine Will brings it forth. What you apparently do, whether it is meditation, prayer, or any of a number of other spiritual practices, is done through you and for you in a way that prepares you for more growth. You can even live without any special spiritual practices. You do not need to go to a teacher in order to hear special talks or receive special energy, although that may happen. Certainly attending Timothy's satsangs helped me. Trust that whatever is appropriate for you will arise without fail. This Absolute Reality is the only real teacher and this is always offering you precisely what will help you the most.

How enlightened someone might be is not really that important of a question since everyone is where the hand of God places them in each and every moment. Furthermore, there is no substantial difference between God arising as an unenlightened person and God arising as an enlightened person. It's just an actor playing a role and the substance is in God the Actor, not the character.

In one case, God is arising as a person who does not understand the True Self and still has some selfish or self-centered tendencies. In this case, God is coming forth as a person who is spiritually asleep, at least to some extent. In the other case, God is arising as a person who fully embodies this wisdom and is always available to express loving kindness and compassion, while dwelling in the deepest joy and peace. Here, God is coming forth as a person who is spiritually awake and free. So all personal consciousnesses (souls) are not "already awake," as you may have heard.

The Key Paradox of Enlightenment

Now, when it comes to your awakening, we discover the key paradox of enlightenment. When your personal consciousness (your soul) awakens, there is the recognition that the personal consciousness is not really you in a fundamental way so you go through an identity shift.

When the personal consciousness is asleep, it holds the idea that it is an autonomous being. When it is awake, it holds the idea that it is an inert collection of phenomena that is dynamically animated by the True Self.

The One Self polishes up the personal consciousness and creates an enlightened person, but that person is just a character (not an actor) in the play of form. So *you* do not become enlightened but *it* becomes enlightened. If you think of yourself as a person (or soul) who has awakened, the personal consciousness is still holding a false idea. You are not fundamentally a person. There is indeed a person and that person may indeed be awake, but the person is not an autonomous self; it is not fundamentally you.

Your "personal self" is not you and it never was you, except in the way that all of creation is you. Yes, in a *profound yet nonfundamental way*, you are everything that has ever been created. As form, you are all form, even though all form is fiction, a fabricated story held by Awareness. As form, you are everything spiritual and everything physical. You are all phenomena; you are all vibration. And yet, your True Self is the vibrationless witness of all vibration. As this formless Awareness, you are that which was never created. Source-Awareness creates, witnesses and dissolves all vibrations.

You are both the totality of created reality and you are the transcendent Source of all of this created reality.

As you take your time to ponder what I offer, perhaps you will begin to see why I like to say:

You are the mountains, you are the rivers, you are the sea. You are the sky, you are the sun, you are the moon. You are all of created reality and yet you are none of that fundamentally.

Fundamentally, you are pure Awareness, Source-Awareness, the Divine Source of everything.

You are the dream and you are the Dreamer.

Enlightenment is the highest and purest set of conditions available for the personal consciousness, but it is not a quality of formless Awareness. This unconstructed Awareness is "unimprovable, cannot regress, need not be purified, cannot be liberated, and need not be awakened," as Timothy often reminds us. And this is what you are. This is what enlightens all personal consciousnesses even though Awareness itself cannot be or become enlightened.

The Mind and the Ego Are Not the Enemy

I once heard someone adamantly proclaim in front of a large group, "The mind is the enemy!" Many people say that in order to wake up spiritually, you need to have your heart win its battle with your mind. But please consider this. Your mind holds ideas, and your heart holds emotions. Your mind can hold true ideas or false ideas, and your heart can hold hatred and fear, or love and peace. At the deepest level, only false beliefs, which are very effective habitual hypnotic thoughts, can prevent you from being at peace. There is no battle where your heart must triumph over your mind. Instead of a battle, think of it as the pursuit of truth, love and peace. Work towards tuning your mind into the truth and your heart into love and peace.

As I mentioned at the beginning of this chapter, to fully integrate this spiritual wisdom, both your mind and your intuition must work together. So let's not make our minds the enemy especially since you cannot function in the world without one. And by the way, the purer the mind, the more loving the heart.

A similar thing can be said about the ego. There is no need to erase the ego, as some people seem to think. First of all, very quickly, what is the ego? Well, in large part, your ego is your understanding of who you are as a person, and this includes your idea of how you fit into the world. And an ego is surely required for you to function in society, just like your mind.

But there is another common definition which says that the ego is the part of you that is entirely focused on being selfish and self-centered and this is why so many teachers go on and on about how the ego is the source of all our problems and that it fears its own annihilation. But there is no such part of you. Selfishness is an attitude held by the personal consciousness, that's all. But no matter how you understand the ego, you can be sure that you do not need to be selfish or self-centered to function in the world.

By the way, when it comes to selfishness, let's be clear. There is a big difference between self-love and selfishness. Getting a massage is certainly not a selfish thing; it is an expression of self-love, just like eating good food and thinking positive thoughts. Likewise, being happy is not selfish. In fact, it's easier for a happy person to be a loving person. Selfishness comes forth in both attitude and action when there is a lack of concern for the well-being of others, outright disrespect, or even abuse and hatred. While we of course want God to purify our personal consciousness by removing our selfish tendencies, our healthy ego will not be erased in the process.

The false beliefs that are held by the mind along with the resultant fear, selfishness and self-centered tendencies that are integrated into the personal consciousness are what lead to so much suffering. I can assure you that God did not create you with a built-in enemy or an intrinsic source of problems.

Other Potential Misunderstandings

Some teachers emphasize the common misunderstanding that there is no self at all or that "there is no one here." But there most certainly is "someOne" here; God is here! The One Self of all apparent selves is arising as you, me and "everyOne." *When this is overlooked, the most profound stimulus for genuine loving kindness will be missing.*

This problem came about because of a poor translation of the word "anatta." Originally "anatta" was used by Buddha to point out that each component of the person is "not me" or "not [my fundamental] self," in a way that is similar to the idea that the character is not fundamentally who the actor is, even though the actor and the character are one. Yet anatta was later incorrectly translated as "no self" rather than "not self" and then used outside of its original context of the process of disidentification.

To say in general that there is no self (or "no me") is to say that you do not exist. Yet you know you exist; this is obvious. So you know that there is a problem with this translation. But this doesn't stop people from repeating that there is no self. You also hear that there is no person, or no soul, or that you are not your body. The truth is that you *are* your body, but not in a fundamental way. The mistranslation of anatta as "no self" plays a big part in how all of this confusion started and why it continues today.

Here's what I like to say: Your *fundamental identity* is the One Actor, this uncreated, formless Divine Essence, Source-

Awareness. Your *nonfundamental identity* is the totality of created reality: the stage, the props and all the characters. This is what you are through the process of creation. And your *functional identity* is the combination of the One Actor and the single character (this person) you appear to be.

So first, you disidentify from the person while clearly identifying as Source-Awareness. And then you reidentify in a profound and yet nonfundamental way as everyone, including the person you appear to be.

So you disidentify from the small and reidentify as the All.

All of this is thoroughly divine since God is not merely infinitely intimate with all of creation, God *is* creation. It is God who is arising as everyOne and it is God who is doing everything. How wondrous!

Some people say that God is impersonal yet Timothy likes to say instead that Source-Awareness is "supra-personal." This word "supra-personal" emphasizes that God lives as every person while also transcending all persons. The divine essence of all persons is why there is so much richness in our relationships when we share the One Love of God.

And notice that each person is unique. Here we are talking about the form, not the essence. Just as an actor can play many completely different characters, the One Actor is simultaneously playing the role of each and every unique person. So in form, one person is not the same as another. But of course, in essence, they are One.

Another thing that I hear is that the world does not exist or that it is unreal. This seems to come from a mistranslated quotation from Shankara, who was a highly respected and influential Hindu who lived about 1,200 years ago. In the Hindu tradition, Brahman is the Ultimate Reality underlying all phenomena and Shankara said something like this:

"Brahman is real. The world is unreal." And then he finished with this puzzling statement: "Brahman is the world."

But that second phrase is also offered as "The world is an illusion." Ah, yes, this is a much better translation. This means that the world exists in a deceptive way. But when people think that an illusion is something that does not exist at all, well, we have a serious misunderstanding.

Timothy commented on this subject on his web page titled, "Nondual Spiritual Awakening, Its Source and Applications:"

> *With the dawn of true knowledge, vidya or vijnana, comes the realization, expressed in Shankara's well-known verse: "Brahman alone is real, the world is appearance, the self is nothing but ("disguised") Brahman." (Brahma satyam jagan mithya, jivo brahmaiva na parah). The experience of a world of multiplicity is "subrated" or "contradicted" (badha) by realizing there's only Brahman. In Realization, it is clear that the ordinary world and "jiva"-self, are misperceived —the Truth is Shiva, God. The soul's Real Identity is Divine: "jiva is Shiva." Everyone and every phenomenon in the cosmos is none other than Brahman.*

All this talk of what is real and what is unreal can make your head spin. But it's really not so hard to understand. Let's take the easiest question first: What is unreal?

I like to use an example that is meant to be humorous to help you remember it. Here it is: The pink elephant in your pocket is unreal. It does not exist. Yes, of course, you are now thinking about a pink elephant in your pocket, but that is just a thought and it only exists in your mind. And still there is no pink elephant in your pocket. That is completely unreal. It does not exist. This is very simple.

If people think that the world is not real, they might think that nothing matters and become cold and callous. This might even lead to heartless abuse of other people. The full teaching is this: Nothing matters in an absolute sense since all of creation is a temporary construction, yet everything matters since creation is experiential real and all of creation is fully divine. How could that which is divine not be precious? How could God not matter?

So we see that the full truth opens the heart while an incomplete teaching can lead to a closed heart.

The metaphor of the the actor and the character is quite rich so let's go a bit further with it now. Let's say that an actor is playing the role of a doctor. And suppose you actually need the help of a real doctor. Would you go to this actor to get the care you need? No, of course not. He's just a fake doctor.

But let's look carefully at what is going on. When the actor takes on that role, he really is the character, he really is a fake doctor. He is not pretending to be a fake doctor, he is a fake doctor. And he is using that character to tell the story of the play. Since this character exists, we say it is real. But it exists in a deceptive way so it is an illusion.

Not only does the actor want you to think that there is a real doctor present, but he also wants to hide the fact that he (as an actor) is involved. The actor wants to present the character in a way that makes it seem as if the character exists all on its own, without the substance of the actor. He wants it to appear to be more real than it actually is, so to speak. So again, this is a deceptive presentation.

Now consider this. When Source-Awareness arises as a doctor, the acting is so good that we really do have a doctor who can actually help you. Pretty good acting, eh? And since this Actor is completely imperceptible in every way, the actor is well hidden and the illusion is very convincing.

And here is a very subtle but important point. God is not merely *pretending* to be each and every person, God *is* each and every person just like the actor is not *pretending* to be the character, the actor *is* the character.

What we have in our world is a play that hides the fact that it is only a play better than any play we have ever seen. Not only is God the One Actor who is playing all the characters, but God also arises as the stage and all the props. And finally, God alone is witnessing this spontaneous play from the perspective of each character. The characters provide the audience in this amazing improv theatre! And since God is invisible, the play appears to exist all on its own. We see the story but we can't see the creator of the story.

You are wearing a mask (your body) and looking through the eyes of that mask. When you look into a mirror, it seems that you prove to yourself that you exist fundamentally as a separate, mortal, sentient being. Yet you exist fundamentally as the invisible, formless Source-Awareness looking through that mask. The mask is real. It exists in a deceptive way, so it is an illusion. God arises as what seems to be only a non-divine, mortal person but the truth is that the person is fully divine on every level. It has its mortal body, its immortal soul and its formless essence, *all fully Divine*.

God and Creation – The One and the Many

Next I want to present a table listing some of the phrases that point to God and creation. If you are not comfortable with any of these words, then by all means, use the words you like. There are plenty to choose from.

I do best with English so my favorite phrase for God is Source-Awareness because it presents the two capacities of this transcendent Reality: *the capacity to create*, and *the capacity to perceive*.

Timothy composed a similar list way back in 1991 and posted it on his site in 2006. But I had not seen it until after I compiled my own list. Some of these phrases are frequently used at Timothy's satsangs and this is why there are some identical phrases on both lists. Anyway, I hope you will enjoy pondering these phrases. Here's my list:

God	Creation
The One	The many
Source-Awareness	The objects of awareness
Transcendent Source	Dependent creation
Vibrationless Witness	All vibrations
Infinite Openness	Finite form
Formlessness	Formfulness
Invisible Sentience	Ever-changing sensations
Pure Aliveness Itself	Inert objects
Pure Sentience Itself	Blind objects
Absolute Reality	Relative reality
Fundamental Reality	Nonfundamental reality
Shiva	Shakti
Brahman	Maya
Nirguna Brahman	Saguna Brahman
Reality without qualities	Reality with qualities
Always Awake Dreamer	The dream
The Unchanging One	The always changing many
The One Invisible Actor	The many visible characters
The One True Self	The many apparent selves
The Unconstructed	The constructed
The Story Teller	The story
The Animator	The animated
The Lover	The beloved

Notice that I did not use the phrase "The Void," a term many people really like. This ties in with the word "emptiness," which is the common translation of the word "shunyata" in Buddhism. While these words seem to point to the formless aspect of Source-Awareness, I am just not inclined to use them. But of course if like them, you should keep using them.

Timothy and a few respected Buddhist scholars think that a better translation of "shunyata" is "openness" and this of course points to the open capacity for experience that you fundamentally exist as. So I don't think of myself as empty or emptiness, I think of myself as this openness.

How do you feel when you think of yourself as "The Void"? Compare that to how you feel when you think of yourself as this open capacity for experience or pure, open Awareness. Just take a minute to meditate on each of these and perhaps you will see what I mean.

Notice that both "The Void" and "emptiness" do not point to the two capacities of Source-Awareness. This is such an important flaw that I don't think these words are very helpful for newcomers and this is why I don't use them.

Along these lines, I want to talk about what is meant when people say that something is empty. Usually they mean that the thing they are talking about – a table, for example – has no substance. But the deep truth is better expressed by saying that the table has no substance *of its own*.

It certainly has substance since I can knock on it with my knuckles. All things have substance. Even a nighttime dream has substance since we can perceive it. But all of creation is lacking any substance of its own. The substance that is present is the substance, or essence, of Source-Awareness.

The metaphor of the actor and the character clears this up very quickly since we easily see that the character has no substance of its own, and instead, the substance of the actor is presented to us as if it were the substance of the character. The moonlight metaphor can also help us here since none of that light originates with the moon. Instead, the sun is the source of all that light, which then bounces off the moon.

I hope both of these metaphors help you see why I like to say that all form lacks its own substance rather than saying all form is empty.

Note that when it comes to our formless Supreme Reality, some people apply both the words "empty" and "emptiness." I certainly would not say that Source-Awareness is empty since it is not lacking its own substance. Instead, this substance is completely imperceptible. Now, as far as the word "emptiness" goes, I just don't think it works very well in pointing to the formless aspect of Source-Awareness.

And this brings us to a quotation from the Buddhist Heart Sutra: "Form is emptiness; emptiness is form." Personally, I don't think that the connotations of this saying are as clear as they could be. In my opinion, it is trying to say that Source-Awareness (Openness rather than Emptiness) miraculously arises as everything (all form) without stripping this form of its inherent divine nature. In this way, formless Openness and form are One. But that point is not easy to understand from that short quotation.

I personally think that trying to create a simple saying that offers something like "A is B; B is A" will almost for sure cause confusion.

For example, consider this one: God is creation; creation is God. What would people think if they heard that? Although it's true, it seems incomplete to me since it does not clearly reveal the transcendent source nature of this Creator, or the dependent nature of creation. And it might even make it seem like creation has its own creative powers, which it does not. This is not a circle. God is the source of creation; it is not the other way around. Again, think of the actor and the character.

You may have noticed that I seldom use any Sanskrit or Pali words in my writing. This is because my foreign language skills are just not strong enough for me to do so. This is why learning anything about Buddhism or Hinduism was just too difficult for me until I met Timothy. His language skills are excellent and anytime he used Sanskrit or Pali words in our meetings, he would always tell us immediately what those words meant. This was very helpful for me even though I could only remember the English, not the Sanskrit or Pali. If you are like me, perhaps you appreciate being able to learn about this wisdom without learning another language.

By the way, I don't even call myself a nondual teacher. Yes, when you get right down to the core of what I teach, it really is nondual wisdom but that phrase has been co-opted by a group of people on the Internet who just don't teach what I teach so I don't use that phrase very much. Instead, I just call myself a spiritual teacher who likes to talk about spiritual awakening and enlightenment in simple, clear English. I hope many people will find this helpful.

Teachers

When it comes to evaluating how enlightened a particular teacher is, I would not look at how many people they can draw into a weekend retreat or how gifted they are at getting people high on spiritual energy. Instead, I would look at how humble they are and how much compassion and kindness they offer to everyone they meet. And of course, I would also look at what they teach.

Obviously no one's perfect, but if they frequently lack genuine kindness and compassion, then they most likely also offer an unbalanced teaching. The lack of kindness and compassion can lead to an unhealthy relationship with their students since the students might be treated like objects and possibly exploited for "ego stroking," free labor, money or sex. And an unbalanced teaching can harm the students further since they might adopt this teaching and suffer from the lack of wisdom that is truly liberating and wholesome.

The question of who is best qualified to teach deep spiritual principles reminds me of the Bible verses found in 1 Corinthians 13:

> *If I speak in the tongues of men or of angels, but do not have love, I am only a resounding gong or a clanging cymbal. If I have the gift of prophecy and can fathom all mysteries and all knowledge, and if I have a faith that can move mountains, but do not have love, I am nothing.*

So it is no surprise that all the divine virtues such as loving kindness, compassion, joy, peace, humility, generosity and patience are the guiding light for every genuine teacher and these virtues will be spontaneously expressed more and more through you as this wisdom becomes more and more alive within you.

Now that we have covered the first aspect of enlightenment, let's start our exploration of the second aspect, which is being engaged in the world without being entangled by selfish or self-centered desires and tendencies.

Chapter 10 – Mystical Optimism – How to Glow with the Flow

I've heard it said that optimists live longer and enjoy life more fully than pessimists. And you know what they say about pessimism: it wouldn't work anyway.

Of course I whole-heartily encourage a positive, cheerful attitude since it immediately creates a more enjoyable experience of the moment, and yet in this chapter, I'll talk about an attitude that goes even deeper than just ordinary optimism. I call it "mystical optimism." Let's see what I mean by that.

A Positive Attitude Is Instantly Rewarding

In 2008, I read the book *Pollyanna* by Eleanor Porter, which was published way back in 1913 and quickly became an enduring sensation. In it, we learn how eleven-year-old Pollyanna truly cares about all the people that she meets and how she teaches them to find joy in unappreciated aspects of their lives.

Yet many critics misunderstood Pollyanna's approach towards life and dismissed her attitude as completely superficial and totally without any merit. In fact, this misunderstanding was so prevalent that the word "Pollyannaish" was introduced into the lexicon as a silly attitude that is unreasonably optimistic. The name "Pollyanna" itself was defined as a naive and annoying person who blindly lives in a dream world.

Yet in the book we see that Pollyanna knows how to dig into the circumstances of the moment in a way that often finds something to be genuinely happy about. Slowly but surely, other people around her learn that they can do this too.

Notice that she finds something about the situation to be glad about, which is quite a bit different from choosing to be happy about every aspect of everything. In fact, Porter herself pointed out this difference when she said, "I have been placed often in a false light. People have thought that Pollyanna chirped that she was 'glad' about everything. [...] I have never believed we ought to deny discomfort and pain and evil; I have merely thought it is far better to *greet the unknown with a cheer.*'"

Ah yes, of course, it's far better to greet the unknown with a cheer and once you get the hang of it, you, too, will see how well this works.

And I'd also like to underline the point about not being glad about everything just a little bit more. In the book, Pollyanna says to her adult friend upon hearing of the passing of her aunt's cousin, "[it] must be that there are some things that 'tisn't right to play the [glad] game on – and I'm sure funerals is one of them. There's nothing in a funeral to be glad about."

As far as somber things like funerals, I agree that you shouldn't hold a flippant, game-playing attitude, yet I do think that it can be wholesome to look for beautiful aspects in everything that arises.

When my father passed away, we had a memorial mass for him. The church was packed with over 200 people, even though it was a Monday morning and most people would have normally been at work or school. People came from thousands of miles away. They were all there to offer their love and support for my mother and our family, and to tell my father in unison yet again but not for the last time how much they all loved him. I knew that there was going to be lots of singing and since my talented sister had been overseeing all the music in our church for decades, I knew it would be very beautiful. My sister has a gorgeous voice and on this day, she was sitting with the family and not up in the front of the church as she normally would have been.

When the musicians started playing their instruments for the first song, it sounded wonderful. And when the singers sang their first note, with my sister sitting right behind me singing full voice, boy, did I cry. My sister put her hands on my neck and shoulders to comfort me. This emotional release was completely natural and not something to be avoided. As we saw in the chapter about Tookie, sometimes experiencing deep sorrow will wake someone up to their true nature, this awesome Source-Awareness that gives birth to everything. So even though I certainly would not say that I was glad my father had passed away, I was still able to appreciate not only all the love and beautiful singing, but also the profound emotions that flowed through me.

Pollyanna's kindness, compassion and wisdom are the main reasons why I strongly recommend this book, which you can read for free on the Internet. Pollyanna's attitude has tremendous power and it is available to everyone at every moment. It is a delight to watch Pollyanna's love shine brightly on everyone she meets, and you may even shed tears of joy when you see people release their stubborn grip on their unhappiness and move into their natural state of joy and kindness. Yes, of course, *this* is our natural state. Our human nature is not fundamentally unhappy or selfish.

Give It a Try Yourself

You can test the power of your own thoughts and attitude for yourself at any time. As many teachers have discussed before, when you emotionally accept the present moment, you will immediately create a more comfortable experience. Your inner turmoil will be reduced as you lessen your emotional pushback against "what is."

And here is a very important point:

You are not saying that everything is perfect or that you love everything. You are just flowing along in your life without any hatred; that's all.

When you emotionally reject some aspect of the present, you will immediately experience frustration, anger or some other emotional discomfort. This is what hatred does. Yet you can instead just hold every aspect of the moment gently and honestly so that you can truly know what it really is, and then simply accept it with emotional neutrality.

Do this without adding an extra layer of thought about what society says your experience should or should not be. While the outer circumstances of your life can sometimes seem difficult to accept, they do not hold the power to determine your emotional state of being. So always ask yourself "Am I pushing away with a harsh, judgmental attitude, or am I pulling in with needy desperation?" When you gently hold all that life offers without any urgent pushing or pulling, your life will be completely transformed.

Similar things can be said about the past. While it seems natural to believe that no one can change the actual events of the past, you can indeed change how you presently feel about those events by choosing to accept them or reject them in each new moment.

Some pessimists view the past and the present wrapped together in a way that creates for them the illusion of an inescapable prison. They might think "Disastrous events have ruined my life beyond repair and here are the reasons why this is undeniably true." Certainly there are some events that can present great challenge, such as parents losing a child or someone acquiring a serious health issue that will be with them for the rest of their life. In this way, many people conclude that the past has been so bad that it does indeed ruin the present, and all of this can make the future also seem inescapably bad. They literally put themselves into this trap, which is filled with what might be called unnecessary suffering. Only they can free themselves from this prison by adopting a new attitude and opening themselves up to the real opportunities that lie before them.

An optimistic or pessimistic attitude about the future immediately creates a corresponding emotional state. No matter if you are thinking of the past, the present or the future, you instantly create an emotional state of being in the present. If you think that the future will be bright, you will feel good in the moments that you hold that thought. If you think that the future will be unpleasant, you will immediately experience frustration, sadness or worry.

Surprisingly, this is true even though no one really knows for sure what outer circumstances the future will bring. But, as I've already mentioned, the most important point is that the outer conditions do not hold the power to determine your emotional state of being. This is up to you via the thoughts and beliefs that you choose to hold.

But obviously, people do not adopt an optimistic attitude simply to feel good in the moment. People want to act now to build a better tomorrow and they want to do so joyfully with hope in their hearts. When joyful optimism is combined with good planning and action, we create the best opportunity to bring forth a better world. While I strongly encourage everyone to do this, I must again point out that there is no guarantee of how things will turn out.

The exact "form of the future" is never really known for sure.

Notice that the amount of suffering only depends on the intensity with which you emotionally rejected the conditions of the world. It does not depend on the difference between what you want and what you have.

I like to use the word "prefer" for wanting something without the emotional charge. If I don't get what I want, I might suffer, but if I don't get what I prefer, I'm still pretty happy. The subject can be the same; it's the emotional charge that's gone.

This doesn't mean that you don't care about what's happening in the world. This is certainly not a lesson where you learn to be happy all the time by simply not caring at all about anything. I am not suggesting that you adopt a cold, heartless attitude and respond to bad news about yourself or others with a detached retort such as, "So what? It doesn't matter! I don't care!" When you hear Buddhists talk about detachment, that's not what they are talking about.

When you learn to not let the conditions of the outer world disturb your deep inner peace, you can put your values of genuine caring and sharing into action without being subjected to disappointment based on the outer results.

So paradoxically, you can work on making the world a better place while emotionally accepting it exactly as it is.

You will be naturally inspired to compassionately and joyfully engage in life and this will all unfold spontaneously. If I am engaged in a wholesomely inspired plan and the rug gets pulled out from under me, that's not a problem since I'm not attached to keeping that plan. I am not attached to either the path or any specific goal. I can emotionally accept whatever comes forth even though it might not be what I thought was going to happen or what I prefer.

So detachment doesn't mean you don't care; it means that you don't place any specific demands on the conditions that arise in the world.

Just as it is wise to let go of demands about the present, it is also wise to let go of demands about the past and the future.

An attitude of acceptance coupled with kindness and compassion allows us to fully participate in the world in a meaningful way while being free from the emotional suffering that comes about when we demand that things be a certain way.

Of course you will still have preferences but they won't be in control of you or your emotional state. You won't be self-absorbed in attachments and aversions, and this is the second aspect of enlightenment that I mentioned in the last chapter. This purification is a long, gradual process so just relax and let it deepen one day at a time.

Before we go to the next section, let's consider two fictional events along with their corresponding emotional responses. First, let's consider the passing away of your beloved dog and the sadness that would accompany this. Second, let's consider someone cutting you off in traffic and the anger that might come from that.

Regarding the first, you might say that although you were sad when your dog died, you experienced this sadness as a beautiful and profound emotion. It arose because you really loved your dog and you understand the wholesomeness of both the love and the sadness that comes from the loss of that love in physical form. Together, they point to the richness and preciousness of life. There is no need for you to try to find a way to prevent this sadness from arising. There is no need for you to become a stoic robot or a person that seems superficially happy all the time.

Now, when it comes to your anger at the guy who cut you off, well, you can be glad that you have the opportunity to learn how to lessen its intensity and perhaps reduce how often anger arises in general. Anger can be seen as a teacher who opens the door to greater wisdom and that wisdom can lead to less anger. So without stuffing the anger back down, but venting it carefully, you can work towards reducing it.

Is the Glass Half Empty Or Is It Half Full?

Now I would like to talk about something that some people call reframing. We have all heard the classic question "Is the glass half empty or is it half full?" Are these phrases really equivalent or is there a benefit in seeing the glass as half full? *And is there even another step up?*

Of course we are metaphorically talking about your life so reframing the glass as half full puts the focus on what you have rather than what you lack and this can be helpful since it allows you to joyfully appreciate what you already have. And this grateful attitude creates a state of openness that allows you to receive even more as time unfolds.

While this understanding is quite helpful, I think that there is yet another perspective that is even more rewarding. I am referring to the all-accepting perspective of the mystic's view, which sees that God *arises as* all of creation. Since I have spoken about the mystic's view in an earlier chapter, I won't go into it here but I will offer the perspective of seeing everything as divine as the most profound reframing available to us.

With this mystical understanding, you can joyously embrace an optimistic attitude like never before! You can glow with the flow and dance with the divine in a way that fills your life with a deep richness no matter what shows up!

For people who are stuck in their unhappiness, the next step is to try Pollyanna's glad game and start finding things to be happy about. For the people who are already good at doing that, I suggest that they ponder their ability to be happy by merely choosing to be happy. I don't think I have ever been happy without first choosing to be happy.

Now, as we saw in the chapter about the passing of Tookie Williams, the goal is not to be happy all the time. The "goal," so to speak, is to be completely natural and recognize that even when there is sadness, there is also a deeper Divine Bliss that holds all human emotions. You do not create this Bliss yet it is always available for you to dwell in.

It is interesting to watch how some people often add an extra layer of belief onto the events that arise in their life. Take for example something like losing a job. People often just react by saying, "Oh, no!" But what about all the good possibilities that might come forth? Why do they jump to "negative" expectations? This subject was presented in an interesting way long ago in the well-known Daoist story about a farmer, his horse and his son. It goes like this.

There was a farmer who had worked his fields for many years with his strong and trusty horse, but one day his horse ran away. Now he would have to do all the hard work by himself. Upon hearing the news, his neighbors came by to visit and offer their sympathy. "Such bad luck," they said. "We'll see," the farmer replied. Early the next morning, the horse came galloping back, bringing with it three more wild horses. "Fantastic! Now you can get all your work done much more easily," the neighbors exclaimed. "We'll see," replied the man. Shortly thereafter, his son tried to ride one of the untamed horses but was thrown off and broke his leg. The neighbors again came to offer their sympathy regarding this new misfortune. "We'll see," answered the farmer. The next week, soldiers came to the village to draft young men into the army. Since the son's leg was broken, they passed him by. The neighbors congratulated the farmer on how well things had turned out. Again, "We'll see," was his response. Sometimes the story has even more events or the farmer replies, "Maybe," or "Good luck, bad luck, who knows?" or he simply smiles without saying anything, but basically, this is the story.

People often think the point of the story is that good things can come from bad circumstances and therefore you should always stay positive in the hope that things will turn out in your favor. Or perhaps instead we should see all things as good, no matter what they look like, so that we can be happy all the time. But this story is really about the peaceful balance (equanimity) that arises when you recognize that nothing is intrinsically satisfying or dissatisfying.

Nothing is intrinsically good or bad; everything is neutral.

You bring your own interpretation to everything and this is what determines your experience. You step back from the roller coaster ride of life when you drop the idea that things are inherently good or bad and simply choose to joyfully engage in life unselfishly, with kindness and compassion for everyone.

Flawlessly Aerodynamic

So how are you doing? We are all asked this question everyday and obviously we all have different things to say about how our lives are unfolding. When people ask me how I am, I often tell them that I am *"flawlessly aerodynamic."* This means that I can flow along with life in a comfortable way without getting my feathers ruffled – that I *"glow with the flow"* most of the time, (a phrase I heard way back in 1987). While I have not mastered this completely, I am always willing to try my best. So perhaps I can inspire you to start reporting that you too are *"flawlessly aerodynamic."* It's fun and can lead to an interesting conversation about the benefits of an attitude that is both positive and open.

Now of course, your friends really do want to know what's going on in your life so when they ask how you are doing, I recommend that you be forthcoming in a way that never portrays yourself as a victim. If there are events that might commonly be judged as bad, just add this: *"I'm not complaining; I'm just reporting."* For example, you might report that your car broke down and you don't know how you are going to get it fixed. But you can add that you might be getting a new one because the old one has fully served its purpose.

Just because you don't know what is going to happen next doesn't mean that you are in the middle of a "negative" experience. Everything can come and go like water off a duck's back. That's another one of my favorite phrases. I often use it when people ask me how I am doing when they know that I am dealing with challenging circumstances. My worries just dissolve and flow away like water off a duck's back.

What I am talking about here is living without placing sharp, emotionally charged judgments upon people, events or things and this reminds me of a funny little story. After a public speaker finished his presentation about being nonjudgmental, he privately asked his videographer, "How was my talk?" The videographer responded with shock and surprise, "You just asked me to judge you!" But actually, that's not it at all. He just asked for an assessment, an evaluation, and that can be quite helpful. What if his talk was disorganized and hard to follow? Surely he would like that feedback so he can improve his talk, and this can be given without any emotionally charged disapproval.

You must be able to clearly and correctly assess the conditions of the world around you if you want to function in a healthy and productive way. Certainly you should discern when someone is angry or unhappy and so forth. It is not "bad" to say that someone is being mean or hateful, if that is the case.

Yet you immediately send yourself into your own personal hell when you harshly judge someone with a strong emotional charge, as if you think God should condemn them to hell. Instead, it is you who goes there straightaway.

This is what "Judge not, lest you be judged" means. It's not that at some point in the future God is going to judge you for judging others. No, not at all. The natural consequence of harshly judging someone is that your own personal experience will instantaneously become miserable. Only you can free yourself from that misery by letting go of judgment.

And when it comes to letting go, *it is paramount to recognize that letting go is always completely and absolutely effortless!* It never takes even the slightest effort to let go of something. If something is really heavy, yes, it will take a lot of effort to lift it up. When difficult situations arise, people sometimes say that they have a heavy cross to bear. *But we are letting go, not lifting up!* It is only the fear of what might happen as a result of letting go that keeps people hanging on. But is that fear helping you? Is the unknown really dangerous?

Being happy most of the time just because you can, and being enthusiastic about the wondrous way that your life is unfolding even though you don't know what is going to happen next is one of the most sublime states available to you.

In your dance with the Divine, you never know what is coming next. Will you be spun around, held close or tossed through the air? The aliveness that comes from not knowing cannot be matched, especially if you feel safe, if you don't think of life as dangerous. And when you recognize that everything is in the hands of God and that everything really is for your benefit, this feeling will be automatic. Of course I realize that this belief is indeed very bold but perhaps I can inspire you to try it on for size. You might surprise yourself with what you discover.

Your happiness will automatically inspire you to be kind and compassionate, and the fact that you are comfortable with the uncertainty of life means that you are at peace. You do not need any outer conditions to change because you already see everything as fully divine.

110

And yet paradoxically, you are following your own wholesome inspirations to make the world a better place for everyone. This is a healthy desire; it is not an unhealthy, selfish desire. There is nothing that needs to be fixed yet there is plenty of work to do. And of course, we won't forget to enjoy plenty of play time, too.

A regular optimist sees both the potentially "good" outcome and the potentially "bad" outcome and maintains a joyful, positive attitude while trying his or her best to bring about the "good."

A mystical optimist does all of that yet they understand the outcomes as "preferred" and "not preferred," without any emotional charge. They also know without question that everything that shows up is fully divine and finally, they know that their experience is a reflection of their core beliefs.

This just happens to be the subject of the next chapter so let's see what we find about that.

Chapter 11 – Seth: "You create your own reality!"

Way back in 1980, I started to read some of the Seth books, which were channeled by Jane Roberts. I found Seth to be wise, insightful, compassionate and humorous. I quickly felt comfortable with his refreshing ideas and applied them to my life as best I could.

Key material for this chapter comes not only from Seth, but also from Bashar as channeled by Darryl Anka. And I will cover some important Buddhist and Daoist principles as I learned them from Timothy Conway. I think this broad perspective will help us understand this important topic.

Seth and Bashar offer compatible views about the creative process. Seth often joyously proclaimed, "You create your own reality!" Bashar offers us the idea that the beliefs you choose are the seeds that lead to your emotional state of being. Then your beliefs and emotions work together with the actions you choose to create the circumstances that arise all around you. Those circumstances are best understood as a reflection of your beliefs, emotions and actions. Once you understand this, you will stop trying to improve your life by manipulating your outer circumstances directly.

Now let's take a look at what Seth and Bashar have to say about the scope of your creative power and your freewill.

Working Within Your Chosen Boundaries

In *The Nature of Personal Reality*, Chapter 2, Seth offers this:

> *[If] you believe that you are at the mercy of physical events, you entertain a false belief [an unnecessary limiting belief]. If you feel that your present experience was set in circumstances beyond your control, you entertain a false belief. You had a hand in the*

development of your childhood environment. You chose the circumstances. This does not mean that you are at the mercy of those circumstances. It means that you set challenges to be overcome, set goals to be reached, set up frameworks of experience through which you could develop, understand and fulfill certain abilities.

The creative power to form your own experience is within you now, as it has been since the time of your birth and before. You may have chosen a particular theme for this existence, a certain framework of conditions, but within these you have the freedom to experiment, create, and alter conditions and events. Each person chooses for himself [or herself] the individual patterns <u>within which</u> he [or she] will create his [or her] personal reality. <u>But inside these bounds are infinite varieties of actions and unlimited resources</u>.

The inner self is embarked upon an exciting endeavor in which it learns how to translate its reality into physical terms. The conscious mind is brilliantly attuned to physical reality, then, and often so dazzled by what it perceives that it is tempted to think physical phenomena is a cause rather than a result. <u>Deeper portions of the self always serve to remind it that this is not the case</u>.

Bashar offers us a very similar perspective. Here is how he puts it:

"There are two types of freewill: the freewill of the physical you, the physical consciousness you know yourself to be [and] the freewill of what you might call the higher consciousness, the total being. Now the freewill of the higher consciousness usually will express itself in your terminology as what you perceive as predestination or fate but it only expresses its freewill in that sense in the most generalized of terms. All of the specifics of how you experience the freewill of the higher

consciousness is up to the freewill of the physical being you are in this world at this time.

"[Here's an] analogy [...]. Let us say [that] before you chose this physical life, [when] you were more blended with your higher self, you determined that through and down a specific hallway in this life, you would [travel]. That is your general theme, your general destiny. How you [travel] down that hallway is up to the freewill of your physical being. You can walk, you can run, you can go in the light, you can go in the dark, you can go alone, you can go with friends, you can swim, you can fly, you can go backwards, you can go upside-down, you can look [in] all the doorways [along] the way, you can go right to the end. It is up to you how you [travel] down that hallway, but [travel] down that hallway, you will, because that is the basic experience that the total soul, the freewill of the total being you are, desires to have."

So your "total being" is indeed free to explore whatever it desires though many lives. Yet it has chosen a specific theme to explore in this life and this will come with certain challenges. What attitude will you choose to meet those challenges? Will you choose to live in joy, as best you can, and perhaps even be an inspiration for others? Some of you may know the story of Helen Keller and how she inspired millions of people even though she was both blind and deaf for most of her life.

If you try to go outside of the limitations of your current theme, you might become frustrated or confused. Well, I want to inspire you to emotionally accept the apparent limitations of your life while still working and playing within those boundaries. No one knows ahead of time what will arise when you joyfully pursue your wholesome, unselfish desires. But rest assured that when you adopt a positive attitude, without insisting on any particular outcome, you will avoid most of that frustration. Bashar encourages us to follow our excitement with integrity, by which he means without hurting ourselves or others.

The idea that you have an infinite number of choices within certain boundaries seems impossible but when you think about it, it makes sense. This point is very important and often misunderstood so let's go into it a bit more.

If I ask you to pick a number between 1 and 10, most people will limit themselves to whole numbers and in that sense, the choices are indeed very small. But when you realize that you can pick any number between the two limits, you see that you could pick 2.5 or 3.75. You could even pick pi, which has an infinite number of digits, but it is still between the boundaries. So you have an infinite number of choices even though you have boundaries.

As another example, consider the ukulele, which is obviously a very limited musical instrument. It is very small and can't play very loud. It only has four strings and a modest musical range. Yet I once heard a ukulele virtuoso passionately explain that he had fallen in love with his ukulele precisely because of all its limitations. And, boy, could you hear this love affair come alive when he played! And notice that an infinite number of songs can be played on this limited instrument. What a delightful paradox!

What I am saying here is that even though you cannot do absolutely anything, deep satisfaction is still available to you. So consciously work toward a better future but don't harshly blame yourself if it does not turn out the way you had envisioned. Just accept it as "what is" and move forward.

I like to put it like this:

Joyfully seek what you love; joyfully love what you find!

Many of you know the simple but profound Serenity Prayer:

"God, grant me the serenity to accept the things I cannot change, the courage to change the things I can, and the wisdom to know the difference."

Within the common understanding of our personal self, I think that this is an excellent posture to hold. No one can know exactly what the future will bring. Many situations are like a baseball batter trying to hit the ball. Just do your best and accept what happens.

I know that other teachers say "Don't *try* to do something; *just do it!*" but it seems to me that there is a little more to this. A lot depends on the nature of what you are trying to do. Choose some new core beliefs? Yes, just do it. Learn to sing better? Sure, just do it. Sing in Carnegie Hall? Just try your best and see what happens.

Not knowing what is going to happen is an essential aspect of what makes us feel alive and I think that it is one of the most beautiful things about being human because it creates a sense of adventure, a sense of discovery. And when it comes to your unknown future, remember, God may have a wonderful surprise for you at any moment! If we always knew what was coming, there would never be any surprises.

What would life be like without surprises?

When you grasp the full scope of this wisdom, you see that life is both perfectly safe and yet still very adventurous.

Popular Self-Help Books

Now let's take a little time to examine what has been offered by our popular culture during the last eighty years or so regarding our understanding of our potential as individuals.

One of the most enduring books about this subject is Napoleon Hill's famous *Think and Grow Rich*, which was written in 1937 during the Great Depression. Napoleon Hill himself pointed out in the book that it was meant to be used in a broad sense, not just for financial matters, although that was clearly the central focus. The title promises people relief from their money problems and I suspect that the title was picked by the publisher with the intention of maximizing sales at a time when there were many desperate people. They were happy selling lots of books even though not many readers really got rich. Even still, *Think and Grow Rich* has influenced many authors and motivational speakers ever since it came out.

Hill's book, along with Dale Carnegie's *How to Win Friends and Influence People* (1936), Norman Vincent Peale's *The Power of Positive Thinking* (1952), Maxwell Maltz's *Psycho-Cybernetics* (1960) and others like them, eventually set the stage for something called the Human Potential Movement. It got started in 1962 when Michael Murphy and Dick Price founded The Esalen Institute in Big Sur, California, which was considered the primary center of the movement.

The people involved in this movement focused on finding ways to help everyone bring out the best in themselves, so this was called self-actualization. While Esalen is still there today, the Human Potential Movement, as such, is not receiving anywhere near as much attention as it once did, and many people who were instrumental in its formation and development have passed away. In a general sense, the Human Potential Movement wanted to inspire all of us to improve both our lives and our personalities, and it wanted to give us some effective tools to help us do this.

As the Human Potential Movement became commercially viable by selling self-help books and offering workshops, it inspired several offshoots. Richard Bandler and John Grinder were heavily influenced by the Human Potential

Movement and together they created a tool known as Neurolinguistic Programming (NLP). With a personal annual income of $800,000 in 1980, Bandler's message that "if any human being can do anything, so can you," was proving to be quite lucrative. But is it really true? Although NLP is now falling out of favor and has been discredited in the eyes of some professional psychologists, many of its ideas are still in circulation today, but only some of these are truly helpful.

In the middle of all this, the modern New Age movement was born, although certain aspects of that movement can be traced back much further. Channeling, which plays a big role in the New Age movement, has been going on for thousands of years and has always been controversial. In my opinion, some channeled material is excellent, while other material is quite problematic, just like the work of regular physical people. Jane Roberts started channeling Seth in 1963 and *Seth Speaks*, the first book entirely dictated by Seth, was published in 1972. Seth used the phrase "you create your own reality" throughout his many books and the phrase became a fairly popular slogan of the New Age movement in the 1970s and 1980s.

But it seems to me that this phrase was often interpreted in a way that was much different from what Seth intended and a new phrase was born: "You can be, do and have anything you want." This is usually understood to apply to your life right now no matter what your circumstances are.

I remember a motivational teacher using that phrase in front of a large group of people way back in 1980. While you can find this phrase in many books, it was certainly the focus of *The Secret* (2006), which went on to become one of the most popular self-help books and DVDs of all time.

The claim that you can be, do and have anything you want is like a triple scoop ice cream cone. Yes, "The Be, Do, Have Triple Scoop!" One scoop vanilla, one scoop chocolate, and one scoop strawberry. Who doesn't want that? Marketing this is easy because it promises to quickly end everyone's suffering. It plays right into the hands of the world's simplest and most common philosophy: I will be happy when I get what I want, and *this* is how I get what I want – no matter what! The goal, of course, is to continually create things that match your endless desires, a tall order indeed.

Since health, wealth and romance are the common areas of focus and these subjects are so highly charged with emotion, many people will quickly jump at any potential solution, even if there are a few vocal individuals who say that it didn't work for them. Perhaps they just didn't do it right. Perhaps they let a little bit of doubt creep in and that was enough to ruin the whole thing. And what about all those compelling testimonials? They must have been written by the people who did do it right and it shouldn't be too hard to become one of those people, right? Or so the thinking goes.

Once a book starts to sell reasonably well, big radio and TV shows start to talk about it, which leads to even more sales. The word-of-mouth "buzz" and the low price leads to even more sales. When you add to the mix some very slick packaging and the promise that this will be fast and easy, well, you have a very potent brew for massive sales even if the core message is a misunderstanding of the truth.

When one book finally falls out of favor, another one comes along with the claim that it provides the key ingredient that was missing from the earlier books. In one form or another, this has been going on for a very long time!

But how is all of that working out for you? Well, I am sure that you have noticed by now that you cannot just create anything you want. Are you ready to be honest about that?

In spite of all these points, I do think that you do create your own reality. Here's what I like to say:

No one knows specifically what your beliefs, emotions and actions will create in the world of form, but whatever arises will always match your core beliefs.

Since your core beliefs are at the beginning of this creative process, all effective change will start there. If you desire a more joyous state of being, you must drop the core beliefs that are preventing this joy from arising and adopt beliefs that allow you to be happy right now. Then you will take wholesome actions that correspond to these new beliefs.

If you believe that you are not good enough to be loved, you will feel unloved and your circumstances will seem to verify this belief. Yet even after shifting into a positive belief where you *do* believe that you *are* good enough to be loved, you still will not be able to dictate that certain people will love you in the way that you want. But you will now be open to the love that God will bring you through the kindness of some of the people around you, perhaps in ways that you did not even expect. So you will now have the experience of living in a loving world. What a profound shift!

So the universe is not your personal mail order catalog simply waiting for you to clearly make up your mind and place your order as some people have claimed. This is not about creating specific outer circumstances so that you can then become happy. If you are not happy most of the time, then you must first change the core beliefs that are preventing you from being happy right now.

Your most natural state of being is the one filled with joy and peace. Think about that for a while. And notice that it takes no effort to simply be in your natural state. When you let go of fear, this is what you relax into. And in a very beautiful way, this is the optimum state for God's love to flow through. Again, it is easier for a happy person to be a loving person.

At its deepest level, this is about releasing limiting beliefs such as "I am not good enough to be loved" or "I don't fit into this world" and embracing the core beliefs that *you are good enough to be loved* and that *you do fit into this world beautifully*. This allows you to be open to the changes that God's love, wisdom and power will bring you.

So I am not going to tell you that you can get a new car by visualizing it in every detail or that you can increase your bank account by repeating affirmations that proclaim that the money is already there now. You can try that if you want, but I just don't think that is the correct teaching.

Please don't misunderstand me. I am not pushing back on the ideas offered in *The Secret* and other popular books in order to make you go back to the conventional approach of trying to improve your life by working directly on your outer conditions. Instead, I am inviting you to move farther down the path to a deeper wisdom. Although I don't think that you can be, do and have anything you want in this lifetime, the good news is that you can still live a happy and fulfilling life in your own unique way without getting everything you want. What a relief! And you *can* dwell in this ever-present divine peace, love and joy that is so wholesome and natural.

The process of spiritual liberation does not culminate in the power to create whatever you want. Liberation means that you are free of all selfish and self-centered desires and that you clearly understand that your emotional state of being is your own choice in every moment. This is entirely up to you. All outer conditions are completely powerless in every way. You are never a victim of anything or anyone.

While there are many positive things about the current New Age movement, the misunderstandings about conscious creation are holding a lot of people back. If you are open to a deeper understanding of this important subject, then you are ready to make some real progress.

False Beliefs, Limiting Beliefs, and Negative Beliefs

When we drop a ball, it falls at a certain rate. If someone believes that it will fall at a different rate, that false belief will not change what really happens. If you believe that you can be forever young in your human body, holding that belief will not make it happen. The idea that we can be, do and have anything we want in this lifetime is yet another false belief. Adding this superficial false beliefs on top of the basic beliefs that create the human experience will not change anything.

False beliefs can create confusion or lead to an attitude of denial or create a person who is simply out of touch with the world. So it is to our benefit to weed out false beliefs and create for ourselves a clear understanding of our world.

The idea that we create our own reality is a fundamental law and it is always in effect. Yet if we believe that we do not create our own reality, we will have experiences that seem to prove to us that our false belief is true. Paradoxically, this all comes about because the law is indeed true.

When it comes to our own lives, our observations are often accepted without adequate analysis. We need to look deep enough to see that our core beliefs are at the beginning of the creative process and this process leads to our personal experience and our outer circumstances.

For example, if someone believes that they don't fit into the world, they will simply point to the many ways that their life has demonstrated to them that this belief is apparently true. They use those observations to validate that belief.

But when we experiment with new core beliefs, we see that these new beliefs lead to new emotions, then to new actions and then finally to new experiences and circumstances.

So instead of believing that what we see around us is a reality that exists separately from us, we should recognize that what we believe leads to what we see around us. Again, it is just a reflection.

The belief that you don't fit into the world will create experiences that allow you to explore what life would be like if it were true. These experiences are obviously more restricted than what you would otherwise experience.

I usually call these beliefs "unnecessary limiting beliefs" in order to distinguish them from the necessary limiting beliefs that are required to create our basic human existence in the first place. Yet it is also fine to call these beliefs "false beliefs." You really do fit into the world. How could God create you and then forget to create a place for you to fit in beautifully? This is why Seth calls these beliefs "false beliefs" even though I often call them unnecessary limiting beliefs.

Weeding out your unnecessary limiting beliefs will definitely change your life in a very noticeable way and you can indeed do this with a short daily exercise.

Since you knew about the limitations of physical reality before you made your choice to be here, you consciously chose these limitations. Next, you chose the initial circumstances of your life. Then you chose to forget that you made those choices. Sometimes we choose difficult circumstances because they help our souls grow. These choices are made by your "higher self" which is what Seth calls your "inner self" and what Bashar calls your "higher consciousness."

We have all freely chosen to experience life on the physical plane with the laws of physics just exactly as they are. It's a package deal. Our fundamental limiting beliefs about being human and living on earth include these laws and we chose to embrace them precisely because they allow us to create our human adventures in limitation.

I also want to point out that it is fine to say that a belief is either positive or negative. A positive belief is one that leads to something you prefer while a negative belief is one that leads to something you do not prefer. This is true even though all beliefs are intrinsically neutral at the deepest level.

Examine Your Belief System

In early 2012, I was inspired to read *The Nature of Personal Reality* for the second time. This was when I reexamined my personal belief system and discovered several key limiting beliefs that I had held for a very long time. They had escaped my detection when I initially read the book but now that so much time had passed, it was very easy for me to see how these beliefs had shaped several significant aspects of my life. This is now crystal clear to me.

Seth clearly says that your core beliefs are always in your conscious mind and never buried away in your subconscious mind where they would be impossible to examine. He says your beliefs are like the items in a familiar room where you normally only pay attention to a few items. In that sense, some items seem to be invisible but they are really there just waiting for you to look at them. The point is that you do not need to use a hypnotist or a psychiatrist in order to discover your core beliefs. Instead, you just need to take some time to explore your conscious mind yourself.

Your subconscious mind automatically follows the beliefs that are held in your conscious mind. These beliefs are the blueprint for what the subconscious mind will build. But the subconscious mind is not in control; it just follows the instructions it receives. If you change your conscious beliefs, you change what your subconscious mind builds for you.

You are in control since you are in control of what beliefs you hold in your conscious mind. This is the key.

(Who is really doing this? Recall what I said in Chapter 9 about picking up a pencil. The True Self is doing everything.)

Seth says that our unexamined and habitually held limiting beliefs are like the invisible bars of a prison we have built for ourselves. He says we incorrectly think that these limiting beliefs accurately describe *fundamental unchangeable aspects of reality.* But they are really our *chosen beliefs that lead to our personal experience.* When we realize this, we can choose different beliefs. He adds, "Your thoughts, studied, will let you see where you are going. They point clearly to the nature of physical events. *What exists physically exists first in thought and feeling. There is no other rule.*"

It is very important to note that Seth says that your core beliefs point to the *nature* of your reality. They do not determine any specific set of outer circumstances such as a particular car, home, health condition or relationship. This is why I sometimes say, "You create your own surprises." But of course, Seth's message is more completely and clearly expressed as "You create your own reality."

Notice that the idea that you can be, do and have anything you want is oriented towards specific outer circumstances while the idea that you create your own reality is primarily oriented towards your inner experience, your state of being.

Now, here are the most important beliefs that I found when I reexamined my belief system. Let's start with the ones that have served me my entire life and are still serving me well today.

1) God is always taking care of me.

I remember being in grade school when I first heard the verses in the Bible about God taking care of the lilies in the field. [Matthew 6:25 "Therefore I tell you, do not worry about your life, what you will eat or drink; or about your body, or what you will wear. Is life not more than food, and the body more than clothes? And who among you can add a single hour to his life by being worried? Observe how the lilies of the field grow; they do not toil nor do they spin, yet I say to you that not even Solomon in all his glory clothed himself like one of these.]

While this can be interpreted in several ways, for me at that time, it was very simple. It meant that I would always have a place to live and food to eat and that I should not worry about being taken care of. It was at that young age that I embraced this belief and I have never let it fade.

Of course we realize that these verses do not mean that God will keep the lilies in pristine condition forever since that is not what happens. Living things often grow into an optimum state and then they fade and die. Later they decompose and that material can become part of new living things. In this way we see the natural beauty of all stages, and no stage can exist without all the others. Cultures all around the world, throughout all of time, have noted this continuous cycle of birth, transformation, death and rebirth. It is in this larger sense that everything is taken care of by God.

2) It is easy for me to be happy, even while living a very simple and modest life.

At a young age, I learned by experience that I could be happy without having many material things and this belief plus the idea that God would always take care of me worked together in a way that allowed me to have a solid foundation to stand on, no matter what was happening in my life. In a general sense, I was reasonably happy and well balanced.

126

3) Deep spiritual truth is always available to me.

Throughout my life, I have always had a powerful thirst for the truth and the relaxed and comfortable belief that this would come to me one step at a time, in a natural way.

4) In general, my life is more like a fun adventure than a dangerous and difficult burden.

While those beliefs have always helped me in many important ways, here are the two most important beliefs that were not serving me very well:

1) I did not fit into the world.

2) The "pie" is limited in size and if someone takes a slice, everyone else has to do without that slice.

So let's talk about not fitting in. When I was in grade school, I was almost the shortest boy in my class. During the sporting games at recess, the two best athletes would be the captains and they would take turns picking their teammates. It would finally come down to a few guys that neither captain wanted and one would say to the other, "You can have all those guys." Yep, I was in that group and no one wanted me on their team. In general, I was also pretty shy and did not make many friends.

But in high school, I became a pretty good distance runner and I hung out with the other runners. Yet we were still a pretty shy group and my social life was still quite restricted. This pattern continued through college and as I got closer to college graduation, I had a pretty strong feeling that I did not fit into the technical career that my education had prepared me for, even though my aptitude and skills were very good. This was a significant "problem" to which I had no solution. While I was competent in the subject matter, I just did not have the soul to be a computer software professional in an

8 to 5 world. It was more like I had the soul of an artist but I was not a painter or anything like that. I thought of myself as a free spirit looking for a way to fit in, but not yet finding it.

My belief that the pie was limited and that I did not have a place in the world dynamically interacted with my belief that God would always take care of me and my belief that I could be happy with a simple life. The result was that I chose to step aside and let other people have "that job," "that girlfriend," and "that home." After all, it seemed to me that other people needed those things more than I did. I did not want to hurt them so I did not take the slice that they needed for their own happiness, or at least that's a bit of what I was thinking.

I spent many years living in extremely modest living situations such as a small space in a converted garage or a tiny room in a house, cut off from the rest of the house. I had almost no social life and little work. But I had lots of free time and that was one of the things that I always wanted.

I enjoyed spending lots of time in nature thinking about deep spiritual questions. I certainly wasn't bored. I could go running, hiking or biking as much as I wanted. I did not have to ask a boss if I could go to the beach to play volleyball during the afternoon. My computer password at this time was "freedom" and I used much of my free time to work on several of my own projects. Although none of them resulted in any financial success at that time, this could still change at any minute.

Being able to look back over the last three decades gives me the perspective to easily see how my core beliefs have shaped my life. And it is also clear that I can simply drop the beliefs that are not serving me well. The exact details of what will arise in my life are unknown but it is certainly true that these old beliefs are not required in any way. I *do* fit into the world and it's fun seeing this unfold every day.

Long ago, I tried to improve my situation by thinking thoughts that were meant to attract better circumstances, yet I never removed the core beliefs that were limiting my experiences. When my circumstances did not improve, I simply thought that it was more important for me to learn still more about the spiritual principle of acceptance. I tried my best to emotionally accept my situation while thinking that was the unchangeable framework of my life.

While emotional acceptance is an important principle, there is often no need to continue with unfavorable circumstances. Seth puts it this way: "If you believe, moreover, that you must accept [keep] your difficulties, then this belief alone can deter you from solving them." [Seth's underline.] He also points out that he is talking about fairly common situations and not, for example, illnesses that have been present since birth. He specifically mentioned that as an example of something that needs to be discussed within a much wider context but that is beyond the scope of this chapter.

So why did I believe that I had to keep my situation? Because I had tried to improve it and I continually failed to do so in even the slightest way. And why was I unable to improve it? Because I had not yet removed my core limiting beliefs. I was just laying conflicting superficial thoughts on top of the more fundamental core beliefs. Since I believed that I did not fit in and that the pie was limited, my circumstances were a reflection of those beliefs. Thankfully, once I understood this, I just dropped those limiting beliefs.

By the way, I never thought that money was bad or that all rich people were mean, greedy or selfish. I knew too many nice people who had plenty of money to believe that. And notice that my abundance of free time, good health and fitness could easily come to me without reducing what was available for others. I did not think that there was a limited pie for those things. This was why I was comfortable receiving those things in full measure. Recognizing this was very helpful for me.

The truth is that everything that is needed will show up in service to each individual in alignment with their beliefs. So the idea about letting others have something because they needed it more than me really wasn't helping anyone. I was just unnecessarily limiting my own experience by going without things that would have been beneficial.

Now that we have laid the groundwork, I want you to take some time to examine your own personal belief system and write down what you find. Sit back and calmly think about your life. What has gone well for you? And what would you like to change? Look for beliefs that are active on a deep level. Review the thoughts that frequently pass through your mind. Follow them through to their core beliefs. What do you think about the world and how you fit into it? Do you have a deep sense of belonging and purpose? Take your time and don't worry about what you will find. To polish a diamond, you simply remove what you do not prefer and so it is with your beliefs.

Some Limiting Beliefs

As you work with your inner wisdom, you will weed out more and more of your unnecessary limiting beliefs about yourself, the world and how you fit into it.

Here are some possible examples:

- Life isn't fair
- Life is a constant struggle
- It's hard for me to be happy
- The world is a dangerous place
- At any moment, I can become the victim of either unkind people or unfortunate circumstances
- No one loves me; it is hard to find true love

- I don't fit into the world; there just isn't a job for me
- There isn't enough for everyone
- Money is bad and most rich people are selfish
- Evil, powerful people control the politics and economics of the world and they are preventing everyone else from having a better life
- I've done some bad things and now I won't receive very many good things

And the list goes on and on. Notice that in all these beliefs, you see yourself as the victim. *But you are not the victim of your beliefs, you are the chooser of your beliefs.*

A beautiful thing about both the nondual wisdom and the Seth/Bashar work is that they erase any fear of becoming a victim. You see that the flow of life can contain things that we commonly call "good" and things that we commonly call "bad" but you still see that everything offers you gifts and wisdom, even the tears that water the garden of your heart.

As the weeds of limiting beliefs are removed from your garden, new experiences will arise in your life. These experiences are just reflections of your new wholesome beliefs yet they cannot come forth until the limiting beliefs have been removed. When you love someone, you don't insist that they do everything your way. So it is that God does not insist that you receive the gifts that are offered. But if you are turning these gifts down because you falsely believe that you do not deserve them or that it is more spiritual to get by without them, then a shift towards the truth will bring you a whole new life.

In the nondual view, at the highest level, the hand of God does the planting, the watering, the weeding, and anything else that "needs" to be done. So your personal self has nothing to be anxious about at all. You just gently involve yourself in any way that you find yourself wholesomely inspired.

In this way, you become joyfully open to the unknown, to the mystery of the future.

Don't be afraid of God or what God will bring you. It all serves you. Remember, things don't just happen *to* you; they happen *for* you.

Absolutely everything happens for you. Everything polishes up the personal consciousness and brings it ever-closer to full enlightenment.

Many books about conscious creation focus on bringing specific things or situations into existence. Cars, jobs, homes, health and relationships are just a few examples. It is often stated that you need to visualize and affirm in very great detail exactly what you want. I'll talk a bit more about this in just a minute, yet right now, I want to point out something I heard thirty years ago:

"There is only one prayer and that is the prayer for liberation. To pray for anything else will only bind you further."

When the personal consciousness relaxes its focus on its own life, it becomes more easily used as an instrument by the Self of all selves in ways that are more helpful to everyone. Of course there will still be a healthy concern for the personal self but it will be free from any harmful "me first" tendencies and paradoxically this will automatically bring you anything that is required for you to continue to blossom in ways that are ever more beautiful.

You don't even need to be too concerned about what you might require in the future. Obviously it is often wise to prepare for the future to some extent, but don't worry too much about it. Do what you can and know that whatever you need will show up exactly on time.

An important point is that any special focus on creating self-indulgent riches and so forth is completely unnecessary and would often not be in harmony with your natural path.

Seth's Prime Belief and Some Affirmations

First let's consider Seth's suggested prime belief:
I am a worthy and deserving person.

Notice that this is an open belief about receiving continuous support. It does not focus on any specific outer conditions, which would be stated as a limited or closed idea.

The shift from thinking "I am not good enough to be loved" or "I don't fit into the world" to an open, receptive posture for the love and support from the ever-present divine power without any specific expectation is the most important shift in core beliefs that most people can make.

This is about removing blockages, not pursuing specific outer circumstances.

Here are a few affirmations that I use to do this:

I, Thomas, joyfully fit into the world beautifully.

I, Thomas, open to and receive the continuous support of God's infinite love and power.

I, Thomas, joyfully step forward and receive all that is good for me in harmony with everyone.

I, Thomas, wake up to the dream, let go of fear, and allow God's love to flow through me in miraculous ways.

Seth's Exercise – Embracing Wholesome Core Beliefs

Seth's exercise for embracing wholesome core beliefs is so simple that it might surprise you and it only takes about five or ten minutes a day. You can certainly do this.

Before Seth presents this exercise, he talks about natural hypnosis and he points out that we have all been hypnotized into a certain way of thinking about ourselves, our world and how we fit into it. This happens throughout our lives yet Bashar points out that much of our belief system is in place by the time we turn three. That surprised me. He says that we start telepathically seeking the approval of our parents even before our birth. The influence of our teachers and the peer pressure from our friends and the popular culture also come into play. Our attitudes and values often mimic what's in hit songs, popular movies, hip TV shows and even the slick advertising that makes those shows possible. Not all of this is coherent so we do our best to sort it all out in our own unique way. Notice that even brothers and sisters can develop completely different belief systems.

Once our belief system is in place, most of us reinforce it by constantly hypnotizing ourselves with our habitual thoughts and corresponding actions that spring from the core beliefs that we have chosen. Both the thoughts and the reinforcing actions play essential roles in this continuous process of both helpful and not-so-helpful self-hypnosis. This is why we will use both thoughts and actions to replace our unwholesome beliefs with wholesome ones.

So here's the exercise. It comes from Chapter 16 of Seth's book, *The Nature of Personal Reality*.

For no more than ten minutes a day, concentrate your attention as vividly as possible on one simple statement that captures the essence of your new belief. With your eyes closed, repeat this statement aloud or silently while feeling the depth of its meaning. You might be able to feel this in various parts of your body, including your brain. Try to avoid any distractions, but if your mind wanders, bring your mind's words and pictures back in line with the essence of this new belief.

Seth says that repetition is necessary to establish the new corresponding biological patterns in your body and Bashar also supports this view, particularly with regards to your brain, its structure, and its connection to your higher mind. This exercise does not require a lot of effort so you should not have to strain at all and the more you practice, the more you will improve your ability to concentrate without distractions.

Spending more than ten minutes is often just a way of telling yourself that you believe that you have really big problems that are going to be extra tough to fix. This is an unnecessary limiting belief and Seth advises us to simply do the exercise for only five or ten minutes.

During this exercise, your new belief will be installed in your conscious mind, and it will provide the new instructions that your subconscious mind will automatically follow. This is a lot like installing a new app on your cell phone or a new program on your computer. Once the software is installed, you can use your phone or computer in a completely new way. Notice that you are not changing your subconscious mind directly, you are only changing the instructions that your subconscious mind must follow.

Now, just like it is helpful to repeat the phrase for five or ten minutes, it is also important to repeat the exercise daily. This will help establish the biological changes and get them to "stick." As the inner channels between your brain and your higher mind are repatterned, and as your body and brain adjust to the new belief, you will most likely feel different. You may feel happy for no apparent reason.

Seth says, "You may experience spectacular results at once, but continue the exercise even if this happens." He also points out that you may have to experiment a bit in order to find the proper wording of your new belief. If it doesn't feel right, adjust it or try something completely different, but make sure it is simple and on target. He suggests that three days (at the very least) are necessary before you can tell how effective this has been, based on your emotional state of being. Again, it is important to note that you are looking at the nature of your experience, your state of being; you are not necessarily looking for any specific set of circumstances to come or go.

In my case, the belief that I did not fit in created a set of circumstances that reflected that belief. When I changed the belief, new circumstances arose that reflected this new belief. But I could not have predicted the precise set of circumstances that arose.

But What If It Seems Like It Is Not Working?

Here are some of the reasons why we don't create what we say we want: we are not happy first, we give up too quickly, we are not really dealing with the core limiting belief that is in play, we use an affirmation that is too specific, our actions don't demonstrate that we really believe what we say we believe, and we do not make any adjustments if we haven't seen a shift in the nature of our experience.

I'll talk about being happy first a little bit later so for right now, let's talk about the example of a new action. Let's say your new belief is that you are well supported by God or the universe or whatever word you are comfortable using. Do something that clearly proclaims this to be true and make sure this action is an action that you would not have taken in the past when you doubted that you were supported.

Now don't go out and buy an expensive car or house that is clearly beyond your means. You don't want to create trouble by overextending yourself. But if you usually do not buy vine-ripened tomatoes or nice avocados because they are too expensive, buying them is the perfect new action to take. Even though this is only a small amount of money, this action is significant since it demonstrates your new belief and this leads to other new reflections.

Notice that this action is not being offered to God (or the universe) like you might turn in your homework to your teacher in order to receive their approval or a reward. This action is for you to see. It is the essential, new reinforcing action that validates your new belief. Now you know that God supports you because you see that support with your own eyes. So make yourself a delicious avocado and tomato sandwich! Mmm, one of my favorites!

God Is the Only Creator There Is

Now let's step back far enough to get the big picture from the nondual point of view. Source-Awareness (God) is the only Creator there is; there are no other creative forces or creative entities. Source-Awareness emanates as this dynamic, ever-changing world we see all around us. This is just a type of dream, and it all unfolds through the will and power of God. This divine dream is witnessed by the One Awareness via all the perspectives provided by each and every unique person. And this Source-Awareness is what you truly are, fundamentally. This is your True Self, your fundamental identity. I go into this more in other chapters but for right now, here is the key point:

God creates the totality of created reality in a way that makes it seem as if each person creates their own reality.

Now, even though God creates everything, I will still often speak about you (the person) creating your own personal reality. This is just speaking from the perspective that sees the character doing things on the stage rather than the wider perspective that reveals that it is the actor (God) who is really doing everything. It is okay to speak from this narrow perspective since everyone easily understands what is being said. We do not have to burden ourselves with the awkwardness of only speaking from the wider perspective.

This is why it is okay for me to start my affirmations with the words "I, Thomas." What we have is Source-Awareness (God), the One Invisible Actor, speaking from the perspective of the character (the person). So I am comfortable saying "I, Thomas, open to and receive the love of God" rather than "God opens Thomas and pours the love of God into him." God is polishing up the person by repeating these affirmations through the person and this is why it is fine to speak from the point of view of the person.

When you recognize that you create your own reality, you can consciously put this fundamental principle into practice. But notice that this recognition is simply created within your personal consciousness by God as a thought, which later becomes a belief. So you (as a person) do not really do anything on your own to gain this understanding.

What we have is an apparent "self" that is animated by God rather than a truly autonomous entity. So it seems like the person wakes up and recognizes how this principle works on the personal level – that we all create our own personal reality. And yet it is all done by God.

Since life is just a fleeting dream-like experience, you have no reason to be worried or upset about any difficulties and all fear can fall away. Nothing has any absolute or lasting substance of its own. And yet, it is God who is taking form as everything in the dream, so everything is divinely precious.

This perspective allows you to emotional accept all of life without any pushback against what you dislike or any desperate clinging to what you do like. And yet paradoxically you still lovingly and fearlessly work for a better world in all the ways that you are joyously and unselfishly inspired. In the deepest way possible, this will automatically bring forth what is best for you and also what is best for everyone. So everything matters and we always work for the good, as best we can.

The greatest gift you can give the world is the gift of yourself as polished up by God. So let God's infinite love continue to flow to you and through you, polishing you up in every moment!

Let Go and Let God – The Paradox of Surrender

Seth reminds us that when the conscious mind accepts too many false beliefs, our understanding of the world becomes quite distorted. In particular, if the conscious mind believes that the higher mind is dangerous and untrustworthy, then the conscious mind closes down the communication between the two, which blocks your access to both your wholesome inspiration and your intuitive wisdom since both of these come from your higher mind.

Seth continues by saying, "When this situation arises, the conscious mind feels itself assailed by a reality that seems greater than itself, over which it has no control. The deep feeling of security in which it should be anchored is lost. These false beliefs must be weeded out so that the conscious mind can become aware of its source once again, and open up to the channels of splendor and power available to it." [*The Nature of Personal Reality*, Chapter 2.]

So here we see that personal peace, what Seth calls the deep feeling of security, depends on your ability to fully utilize all of your resources – including your higher mind – and this depends upon healthy beliefs.

It is the intuitive wisdom from your higher mind that calms the conscious mind by teaching it that it does not need to control what is happening in the outer world. But the false belief that your intuitive wisdom is invalid will shut this wisdom off and create a frantic conscious mind trying to control as much of the physical world as possible, a job that it was never designed to do, and most certainly a job that it cannot do. Yet it appears as if it can do it to some extent, which is why we so often just try harder, but with this same misguided approach.

Thankfully, we can simply release the limiting belief that the higher mind is dangerous and shift from the selfish, petty and fear-based motivating factors initially held as so important by our conscious mind to the more wholesome motivating factors that flow to us from our higher mind.

The conscious mind can adopt these wholesome motivating factors and this is often referred to as "surrendering your life to God." But this phrase is really a bit misleading. It makes it sound like the personal self is initially controlling its own life, at least to some extent, and then one day, the personal self decides to let go and let God completely control its life. But that's not really what happens.

The personal self has never controlled anything; it has never made a single decision. God is the only One who has ever made anything happen. This "shift of surrender" is really, at its core, a shift in the driving factors used in the decision making process, a process that is dynamically unfolding in every moment, a process that has always been controlled by God. So it is God who shifts the focus of the conscious mind to the divine inspiration of the higher mind.

Through the mystery of creation, the One Will arises as what appears to be the separate will of each person, the One Mind arises as what appears to be the separate mind of each person, and the One Power arises as what appears to be the separate power of each person. This is how God does everything while making it look like we do things on our own.

So this is not a shift in *who* is driving the car, so to speak, but instead, it is a shift in *how* the car is being driven. When the personal self surrenders (gives up) its selfish and self-centered desires and tendencies, you will find true personal peace and liberation from dissatisfaction.

You become completely free when you release all your selfish and self-centered desires and flow along with your wholesome desires that are ripe with loving kindness and compassion.

Notice that if you are not yet open to your intuitive wisdom, you might surrender to the chaos of the world or perhaps to the unwholesome wishes of others rather than to the wisdom of your own higher mind. If the idea of surrender stirs up some fear, this is only because you have not yet opened up to your innate wisdom and learned to trust it. This is what brings the deep peace of liberation.

Timothy sometimes speaks of the deva-spirits who have learned to create continuous states of pleasure. This is more easily achieved in the subtle realm rather than on the physical plane but the lessons still apply to us here. He points out that these spirits are trapped by their desire for pleasure. They do not know about the deeper Divine Bliss that is available to them and they stay focused on the more superficial states of pleasure. They lack the wisdom that reveals that everything is divine and therefore they do not embrace the totality of reality. This ignorance makes them slaves to their desires; their desires control them. They are not free. They are not enlightened.

Liberation from dissatisfaction does not come from mastering the ability to create whatever you want. All adventures in form are adventures in limitation. Your true freedom is only found when you joyfully follow your own divine inspiration without insisting on any particular outcome. You continually accept everything emotionally while working to make your world a better place, according to your unselfish preferences.

As I touched on in the previous chapter, your emotional acceptance of things can be done without saying that everything is perfect or that you love everything. I certainly would not say that I love war or that I think war is perfect. But pushing back with anger, hatred or fear will only lead to more war. More on this a little later.

Entering the Stream

The Buddha said that in order to enter the stream that takes you (as your personal consciousness) to enlightenment, you must surrender (or give up) three things:

1) You must give up the belief that you are an eternal, autonomous entity that will go to heaven, achieve some final goal, attain a supreme state or condition such as enlightenment or receive some ultimate reward. While the personal consciousness will become enlightened, it is not an autonomous self. It is not what you really are in the most fundamental way.

2) You must give up the unhealthy doubt that your personal consciousness can indeed wake up from the false sense of "me" and recognize the True Self.

3) You must give up the idea that your personal consciousness is in control and acknowledge the Divine Will, both as it arises in your higher mind and as it expresses itself in the world all around you. You must give up any form of

superstitious actions that try to manipulate the world through rituals. You must stop trying to please or bargain with a favor-granting "god" or "universe." This means that your modesty will increase and you will stop trying to draw attention to yourself for your good deeds since all deeds are done by the invisible hand of God.

Doing these three things will defuel the momentum of self-focus but don't expect this to be finished quickly. It is a gradual process. You simply won't ruffle your feathers as much when things do not go the way you want and you will become even more compassionate and respectful of others. The completion of these steps does not indicate full enlightenment, but it's certainly a very good start.

Pursuing Specific Desires

So what about pursuing specific desires? Is that "pushing the river," as they say in Zen, rather than glowing with the flow? Some people joke that Buddhists desire to be desireless. But a better way to put it is that they have a healthy desire to be free from selfish desires. Without desire, there would be no motivation to do anything, including breathing and eating, so obviously it is good to pursue wholesome desires. As I mentioned before, it's not selfish to do good things for yourself. Your love – which is really God's love passing through you – is for everyone, and that includes yourself. So let's now take a quick look at a story with a specific desire.

I met someone recently who told me about a time when she had to deal with some back pain. She went to the doctor and an x-ray showed a very slight fracture. Every night for the next two weeks, she visualized tiny construction workers filling in the crack with strong material. Then she went back to see the same doctor. He took another x-ray and saw that the fracture was gone! It had been healed in just those two short weeks! This baffled the doctor who spent a fair amount of time comparing the two x-rays to make sure that there had been no mistake. So this could have been done by the power of visualization or a shift to a belief in better health. But either way, I don't think this was wrong or selfish to focus on this specific desire.

Buddha started his life as a prince who had every desire satisfied but in the next phase of his life, he became an ascetic monk satisfying only the minimum of desires for food, water and sleep. Neither extreme brought him the peace he was looking for. The easy path of the rich life left him unfulfilled while the path of maximum frugality left him weak and almost dead. It was only when he took the middle path by holding a flowing posture that he reached enlightenment. So it can be with you.

Surrender to your inner wisdom and this will guide you to your healthy, unselfish desires. Use your own good judgment in deciding what to pursue.

Winning the Lottery

You probably won't be surprised to hear me say that most likely, your path won't include winning the big lottery and moving to Easy Street, where all your challenges disappear. Challenges of all kinds, financial and otherwise, are what stimulate your personal growth, just like weight lifting stimulates the growth of your muscles. Without challenges, you will not grow or learn. So all things considered, a big lottery win probably wouldn't serve you right now, anyway.

Yet if you constantly struggle with money and worry about it all the time, then you do have beliefs that can be changed for the better. The desire to win the big lottery often means that you lack a belief in a continuous flow of adequate support. So instead, you might hope for a way to obtain a large amount of money that will last you the rest of your life.

The truth of the matter is that we have all already won the lottery; we are just learning how to cash in the ticket one day at a time.

And as I like to say, *"Don't make money your god; make God your money!"*

In other words, don't worry about having enough money to take care of your needs. Money doesn't take care of you; God takes care of you. Realize that you always have God taking care of you in a way that will benefit you the most. Do what you are most inspired to do, with kindness for all. Be at peace with the present. Be courageous; engage in life fully without fear of the future. Know that you are fully supported in everything that you do. And of course I am not just talking about financial support, but support in every way.

It will seem as if you are opening to more and more of God's love and you will finally see that God's love for you has always been infinite and perfect at each and every moment.

By the way, here's Bashar's definition of abundance: *"The ability to do what you need to do when you need to do it."* And he likes to firmly add, *"Period!"* Notice how this is about "the ability to do," and not about money or material possessions. He also points out that many people think they need something when in fact, it's just something that they want.

Abundance is about what you really need, not what you want.

God created everything and continues to take care of all of creation, including you. God didn't create everything billions of years ago and then abandon it all to chaotic randomness. God did not even abandon the smallest part of creation.

When you were growing in your mother's womb, she did not consciously build your body. It was the hand of God that did that. Then, at the moment of your birth, God did not say,

"Well, I've done my part. It's now all up to you. I'm outta here." God is still fully involved, and you are still fully supported. *You can't get rid of God or God's perfect love.*

When it comes to removing limiting beliefs, you can know with certainty that new core beliefs will bring about new circumstances, even though you won't know specifically what will arise. If you truly establish new core beliefs, there will be a change in the nature of your experience. This is something that only you can prove to yourself.

Now, when it comes to using affirmations and visualizations to create specific circumstances, well, that is not something I am attracted to. I am more comfortable simply nurturing a positive emotional state of being without insisting on any particular outcome.

A Few More of Bashar's Ideas

Bashar often tells us, "What you put out is what you get back." (Your beliefs are reflected back to you.) He loudly proclaims, "This is not philosophy; this is physics!" What does this mean? Well, a philosophy is often a collection of untestable ideas while physics can be demonstrated as true. In this case, the proof comes from your own experience. You don't have to worry at all about whether someone is trying to sell you a bunch of seductive yet false ideas. Reality itself is truly the ultimate authority.

And obviously, this principle is not something that you need to discover or believe before it starts having an effect; it has always been in effect. Because of this, you can immediately start validating this principle by examining your past core beliefs while looking at how they manifested in your life, just like I did. Once you recognize this principle for what it is, you can put it into conscious practice rather than just letting it run on automatic pilot.

Bashar likes the analogy of building a house. Your beliefs are like the blueprint for the house. They are the instructions for the construction of your life and everything will be checked with the blueprint before it is put into place. Emotions are energy in motion, "e-motion." This emotional energy is like the builders of your house and your actions are like the building material. (This metaphor seemed a little odd to me at first but I still like it.) Of course you want quality in all three areas. You want a good design, solid material and competent workers. That way you'll get a well-built house.

Bashar asks, "If you have a line on the blueprint that is out place, or your builders are not really into their job, or the building material is not really up to par, what kind of a house do you think you are going to get and why should you be surprised when it crumbles to the ground?"

If you want to change your life, you can change the core beliefs that are out of alignment with your preferences. Of course, all three components are essential, but your beliefs are the most crucial since your emotions flow in accord with your beliefs, and your actions flow in accord with both your beliefs and your emotions. So it all starts with your core beliefs, which Bashar calls your "definitions."

Your core beliefs are the DNA for the nature of your own reality, but not for any particular set of outer circumstances.

Happiness Is a Choice in Every Moment

Remarkably, we are told not to measure our success by outer circumstances. Bashar proclaims loudly, "Circumstances don't matter! Only [your] state of being matters!" With this, he is of course saying that your circumstances do not control your emotional state of being and that your state of being "matters" (materializes) in the world around you.

And Bashar enjoys emphasizing that you should not be doing this in order to become happy; you have to be happy first.

He puts it like this. If you are looking into a mirror, you must smile first in order to see a smile reflected back to you. Likewise, he says that the circumstances of your personal life are also a reflection and they will change only when you change your emotional state of being by changing your core beliefs. If you insist that favorable circumstances arrive before you choose to be happy, you will wait forever.

But many people instead think something like this: "Hey, I don't want to be happy if I am still poor. I only want to be happy if I am rich." But if you choose to be happy now, no matter what your circumstances are, you will improve your emotional state of being immediately plus you will allow your life to unfold in a way that is more receptive to God's gifts. If you are trying to get a particular thing so that you can then become happy, you are misunderstanding the creative process and you will most likely be disappointed.

So as we discussed in the last chapter, find something to be happy about now. Even though this is conditional happiness, it is a start. Try your best to nurture your happiness by always looking for something to feel grateful for.

I notice that some people say grace before dinner but then they forget to continue in that state of gratefulness throughout the entire meal. Be grateful as you taste every bite. And after you finish your meal, continue in that state of gratefulness as you taste every bite of your life. Pour your loving heart into every moment.

The next stage is mastering the skill of being unconditionally happy. This will unfold naturally. You will discover that *happiness is a choice in every moment.*

When you choose to be truly happy without requiring any specific outer circumstances, then you will know you have really changed your core beliefs about happiness. Note that there is often a delay before there is a shift in the nature of your circumstances and this allows you to prove to yourself that you are not making your happiness conditional on your outer circumstances. This demonstration is a crucial part of the creative process and a key step in the evolution of this wisdom within you.

So the stages are: 1) habitually choosing to be unhappy because things are not what you want, then 2) consciously choosing to find something to be grateful for, and then 3) consciously choosing to be happy in every moment just because you can.

And with all this talk of happiness, I yet again want to point out that it is okay to cry when the tears are genuinely called for in a natural way. While the tears are flowing, you can still dwell in the deeper Divine Bliss that is always available, a Bliss that holds all human emotions, a Bliss that understands the profound beauty of all human tears.

And here's a very important point. When your chosen role in life includes helping the many people who are stuck in fear and confusion, you might find yourself in the middle of the turmoil that is a reflection of their beliefs. So even though you are holding steady in your own inner peace, your outer circumstances may not be as peaceful as you might expect.

But notice that these circumstances really do reflect the bigger picture of a peaceful person who is comfortable going into the chaos of the world in order to help others.

You can easily radiate peace, love and joy while engaging in wholesome, unselfish action. Don't doubt that you can do this.

War

Someone once asked Bashar (paraphrased), "So these wars, we are choosing these wars? This is what we want?" Bashar basically responds by saying that no, war is not specifically what we want and we are not choosing war per se. Instead, we are choosing core beliefs that lead to war without understanding the connection between the two. And there is something about those beliefs that make us believe that they are indeed true and necessary for our survival. These beliefs lead to the inner turmoil that is reflected in our own personal experience and if they are held by a group, they are reflected in the group's experience.

One of the Seth books that I recommend is titled *The Individual and the Nature of Mass Events* and it goes into this interesting question in much more detail. In Chapter 6 of that book, Seth offers us this:

> *Wars are basically examples of mass suicide embarked upon [...] by men who are convinced that the universe is unsafe, that the self cannot be trusted, and that strangers are always hostile. You take it for granted that the species is aggressively combative. You must out-think the enemy nation before you yourself are destroyed. These paranoiac tendencies are largely hidden beneath man's nationalistic banners.*

Now let's consider Bashar's response to a question from a TV host about creating a peaceful world without feeling the need for powerful weapons to protect us. The host asks (paraphrased), "What can we do to create peace and harmony?" Bashar responds, "Recognize first of all, [that] you can begin to teach the following idea to every being upon your world: Each and every individual truly is as powerful as he or she needs to be to create whatever reality they desire without having to hurt anyone else or themselves in order to create it."

Fear and hatred lead to war. The core belief that there are always people planning to attack you and that you must be prepared to fight back leads to war. The core belief that you need to fight for your freedom leads to war. But these beliefs can be dropped and replaced by the belief that your inner peace is up to you. When this belief is embraced without fear, a new world will emerge. Peace comes from loving peace rather than fearing or hating war, as Bashar likes to put it.

So there is no need for any fighting at all. You do not need to overpower or outvote anyone or even convince anyone of anything. At the deepest level, you have never been a victim of anyone or anything. Your experience is your own personal responsibility. Just pick your core beliefs and let things flow naturally from there.

As more people start using the principles of conscious creation, it will be easier for even more people to open up enough to give it a genuine try. But even still, you can only be responsible for your own experience. Simply offer these ideas to others and do your best to be a good example

Highly Skilled Conscious Creation of Specific Circumstances Is Not a Path to Enlightenment

Timothy Conway does not usually bring up the subject of "conscious creation" *of specific circumstances* but when he is asked about it, he is very clear.

Timothy's most emphatic point is that it is not a path to enlightenment. In other words, it is not a path to liberation and it is not a path to understanding the True Self.

He clarifies it this way: "This idea of 'conscious creation' usually presumes a separate 'me' who can create something, but this 'me' is neither real in itself [standing apart from God on its own] nor does this 'me'-sense have any actual power to create – only the One Divine Self manifests anything and everything."

When people become too caught up in creating change, they often overlook that which never changes, the One Source-Awareness. Furthermore, the few people who seem to become skillful at manifesting specific things can easily get trapped in the pursuit of pleasure and excitement. They might become self-indulgent while thinking, "Boy, I sure am powerful!"

But no matter if people are skillful at it or not, they will often put an emphasis on themselves as "the doer" and miss the point that it is all done by God. So when it comes to true liberation, I caution you about getting too absorbed in making specific things happen. Just be joyously open to whatever arises when God removes your unnecessary limiting beliefs.

You know intuitively that there is more to why your life unfolds as it does than meets the eye, and you also know that a fuller experience of genuine satisfaction is available to you. This is why so many people are confident that there is a deeper wisdom regarding this important topic of creating a truly satisfying life. Yet so many of the popular books only offer seductive yet false teachings that overpromise and underdeliver. And oddly, many people are in denial about how poorly those teachings are working for them. While they cling to those false teachings even more tightly, they do not learn to become truly happy, free or more loving.

When this wisdom regarding the creation of a truly satisfying life deepens within you, you see that the key is mastering the art of engaged surrender. You are engaged in life, but not entangled with a self-centered focus. You simply interact with everyone in every situation with kindness while balanced in peace and joy.

Timothy often tells us that there are three levels, all of which are simultaneously true. The third level is our ordinary world with our conventional understanding of justice and injustice, right and wrong, and so forth. This level calls for us to work towards creating a better world in every way that we can. Yet awakening reveals two more levels.

On level two, we discover that everything that is arising is fully divine in both its form and its essence. Everything is happening spontaneously because of the Divine Will and Power, and it is all happening for the sake of the awakening of each and every person. Even suffering and misfortune are necessary ingredients of this divine recipe and therefore they are accepted without any emotionally charged judgment or pushback.

Finally, on level one, there is full and complete recognition that everything that arises is just a type of dream, and that this dream has no substance of its own. On this level, there is only the One Substance, formless Divine Essence.

By the way, "spontaneous" does not mean "random." It means, "chosen in the moment, unplanned." So does this mean that God does not have any plans at all? Well, I think that it's like planning to play tennis on Saturday afternoon. You have a general plan to meet and play but you do not know what will be chosen in the moment.

So paradoxically, you plan to experience what cannot be planned. This spontaneity is what makes the game a fun adventure, as long as you bring along a fun attitude.

The Takeaway

Here I will again focus on Bashar's point about belief, emotion and action being the three components of the creative process.

Belief: Clear out your unnecessary limiting beliefs such as "I am not good enough to be loved" or "I do not fit in" and shift to the belief that "I am a worthy and deserving person." Don't bother creating specific beliefs about specific outer conditions. Simply remove all blockages to God's gifts.

Emotion: I recommend that you nurture the three classic emotional states of peace, love and joy. The Buddhists like to expand "love" into "kindness and compassion" so they have four states, which they call the four divine abodes or the four radiant abodes since these qualities radiate out into the world.

Action: With unconditional love for all, take action in every way that you are joyfully inspired. Remember that a goal is just a guiding thought that can be changed at any time. Act without any expectations whatsoever and with complete acceptance of everything that shows up.

As you get a better handle on this, you (as a person) will be open in a way that reminds me of the unbounded openness of Absolute Awareness and your divine adventure will unfold with profound beauty and ease.

The state of being that radiates unconditional peace, love and joy at all times, without requiring any specific outer condition is what is meant by detachment.

Detachment is not about cutting off your involvement with the world. Instead, you are involved in the most loving way possible.

I'd like to end this chapter with an ancient short story.

A man lived alone in a very simple hut and one day, he walked into town to do some errands. After many hours, he finally walked up the path to his hut under a dark sky and a silvery moon.

When he went inside his home, he realized that someone had come while he was gone and taken every single thing that he owned. They even took his wooden bowl which he used to eat his rice. He decided just to sit quietly in the middle of the dirt floor and close his eyes for a few minutes.

When he opened his eyes and looked out the window, a short poem came to him:

> *The moon in the window,*
> *the thief had left it.*

~ ~ ~ * ~ ~ ~

That which is most important can never be taken from you because it is you. Yet it is often overlooked because it is both invisible and covered with other things. When everything else is gone, it alone remains.

You are the eternal Divine Awareness, that which creates and witnesses all of creation.

Chapter 12 – A New World: Our Shift from Competition to Cooperation

Hey, Do You Want Some Help?

You've been working for a few hours under the hot sun digging an irrigation ditch for the orchard. It's hard work and there is much more to do but you can handle it. All of a sudden, from out of nowhere, a friendly voice calls out, "Hey, do you want some help?" You look up and see a strong young man smiling down from the ridge above. He even has his own shovel. It's a simple question. What will your answer be?

In a healthy society, that's easy. "Yes! I'd love some help!" The more help there is, the sooner the work will be done. Then everyone can go back to their families, play with their children, make dinner, listen to music and enjoy a nice evening. Tomorrow will be another day.

But what will the answer be in an unhealthy society? That's also easy. "NO!! I'm makin' forty-two bucks an hour! With enough overtime, I figure I can make over a hundred grand this year. I've got a big mortgage, two car payments, and three kids all getting ready for college. I certainly don't need anyone cutting in on my action, so beat it!"

When the offer of a helping hand is pushed aside out of fear or greed, you know you've got trouble on a fundamental level. Yes of course, I certainly understand that communities all around the world have many volunteer groups that would never turn away a helping hand. But what I'm talking about is a society where all the work is shared in the spirit of genuine concern for the well-being of both the individual and the group.

All throughout history, we find examples of cultures that didn't charge money for food, housing, or clothing. All that was just taken care of by a group effort. Sure, many cultures traded items both internally and with other groups, and in that sense you can say that they had a free market where goods of equal value were exchanged.

But still some cultures had a solid foundation of communal sharing where essential items were freely provided. These people did not have to worry about unemployment, home prices or saving for retirement. Of course they were concerned about their crops, hunting, the weather, and perhaps war, but they were not worried about inflation or an economic collapse.

In a healthy society, everyone shares all the work and all the benefits of that work. In an unhealthy society, individuals not only compete for the jobs, but they also compete for the ownership and control of many things, the fruit of which they keep for themselves. Greed, corruption and monopolies can make matters even worse. Obviously, this creates the rich and the poor.

The ultimate outcome of a competitive system like ours is demonstrated by the board game Monopoly. It seems to me that the intention of the game was to make the huge flaws of capitalism obvious to everyone, even children. The details of the origin and intended economic or moral message (if any) of this game are not clearly documented yet it certainly looks like the final outcome of each game is always the same.

As you know, the game usually starts off with six to eight people, each with the same amount of money and no one owns any property. That seems fair enough. Yet after hours of playing, the game is often stopped with only one or two people owning all the property and having all the money. Everyone else has gone bankrupt and forced out of the game. That doesn't look like a very good system to me.

In the United States, less competitive systems such as "socialism," "communism," or "collectivism," are all lumped together and condemned in one stroke. And people often "prove" that these systems don't work by talking about Thanksgiving and the pilgrims at Plymouth Rock. Let's see what we can learn from this story.

Basically we are told that in 1620, the pilgrims faced many serious challenges upon their arrival in the New World. Governor William Bradford kept some historical notes and from these we see that the group was initially organized as a collective. Everyone was expected to work at a level that matched their ability. They would farm, fish, hunt and gather, and the food was to be shared by everyone.

But the motivation of the workers was low. Many men did not want their work to benefit lazy men, and many women did not want their chores to support anyone but their own family. People even resorted to stealing. The overall result was a disaster. Since not enough crops were planted and hunting was not very productive, starvation took its toll.

After the group was almost completely decimated, Bradford changed the social structure to private ownership with a free market for fair exchange. Each family got their own land, and whatever they produced from that land or gained from hunting and gathering was theirs to keep or trade. Now everyone was much more motivated and there was plenty of food for everyone. That is the core of the story. If you want more details, just search the Internet for William Bradford and Thanksgiving.

So does this prove that sharing doesn't work? Well, certainly under the conditions that existed at that time and place, the sharing model did not produce abundance, but that doesn't mean that sharing is fundamentally flawed.

What you need for vibrant productivity is a match between the way the community is set up and the way the people are thinking.

Initially, Bradford set up a sharing social structure but the group did not have a sharing mindset. This mismatch was dysfunctional, as revealed by the lethargy, the stealing and the poor productivity. When Bradford changed the social structure to an "I did it, so it's mine" structure, it matched the non-sharing mindset of the people. This match is what stimulated the productive activities, not that particular economic model on its own.

I think that if a sharing mindset is already held by most of the members of the group, then a sharing social structure will result in even greater productivity, along with the important bonus of greatly reduced stress. After all, what is the real cost of the anxiety that many people today experience in our highly competitive world? Please note that I am talking about genuine, freely given, heartfelt sharing, not forced redistribution of personal wealth by taxation.

This constant worry has a tremendous impact on the health and financial well-being of millions of people. Wouldn't this anxiety be drastically reduced if everyone knew that the entire group would support each and every individual or family as much as possible, like a huge safety net? When I talk about improving our quality of life, I am not only talking about living in nicer homes and so forth, but I am especially talking about replacing the experience of constant worry with the experience of personal peace. *This* is a much higher quality of life!

By the way, I think that people who have a sharing mindset often have trouble staying motivated in a highly competitive society like ours. I know plenty of people who aren't driven to accumulate more and more money. They are much more comfortable building a better world for everyone, and that is what they do, as best they can.

I think that we should celebrate the uniqueness of every individual and not make assumptions about who someone is or what they can do based on their age, gender, education, race, experience, financial status and so forth. We each have something special to give to the world and that gift is our own wondrous self. We should respect everyone but not idolize anyone, no matter what they have achieved.

When we as a society learn to hold every individual as precious no matter what their faults are, no matter how far they've fallen down, when we all cooperate and help one another when one of us is in need, we might not have a perfect, pain-free world, but we will have a world as near to paradise as we can create on this physical plane, the plane with both joy and pain, the plane with both loss and gain.

And we *can* learn to hold everyone as precious. Mothers and fathers will always remember the preciousness of their newborn child. When each of us was born, we all embodied a unique, astounding expression of the divine creative force. What a miracle! *And we are all still that miracle!*

We all deserve respect and appreciation, not because of what we've accomplished as individuals, but instead, because of what we are. We are all in our very essence this eternal Divine Source-Awareness. This never goes away; this never changes.

You are not simply connected to God, every aspect of your being is divine. God is not just deep within you at a special place, you are divine at every level.

So how do we create a society where most people have a sharing mindset? More on that in a minute.

~ ~ ~ * ~ ~ ~

You're sitting in a small outdoor café enjoying some lunch. Even though the meal is delicious, some nearby workers catch your eye. What they are doing seems very odd to you but no one else seems to notice. One guy is digging a hole, and then the other guy is filling it in. Then the two of them move down the street twenty yards and repeat the digging and filling. Finally they get close enough for you to ask about the purpose of their work. They both smile and one of them quickly points out that it does indeed seem silly but there really is a good explanation. The other one chuckles and says that there used to be a third worker who would plant a small tree in the fresh hole before it was refilled. Then they both roar with laughter and add that due to cutbacks, that person lost his job!

So how much of our economy is just busy work? Diggers and fillers just doing their job because that's what's been funded even though there is no real benefit to society? How many jobs would just flat out disappear – in a good way – if the economy were based on sharing. If you needed a house, it would be provided. If it burned down, it would be rebuilt without any questions about whether you had insurance or enough money. The simple fact that you were alive earned you the right to have a home, food and clothing. No cash or paperwork would be needed.

With this direct approach, the total workload on our society would be lower and everyone would have a lot more free time. We could have a fuller and richer life. This reminds me of something that Pollyanna said shortly after she moved in with her aunt. Her aunt had scheduled Pollyanna's summer days and evenings with so many responsibilities and activities that Pollyanna protested that she did not even have enough time for "just living." How many people feel that way today?

When I was a young child, I did chores for my family. You know, watering the lawn, mowing the lawn – that kind of thing. Once my chores were done, I could go play. In other words, once I became unemployed, I was free to do other things. So in this sense, unemployment was a good thing. Now of course if other tasks came up later, I would take care of them, but again, everything would be done eventually.

Now, if society at large ran out of things that needed to be done, we would all be unemployed and we would all be free to do other things, right? And this would be a good thing, of course, because that would only happen when everyone's needs were taken care of, as best they could be. This is obviously an oversimplification since living in the physical world takes continuous physical work, so we will never really be done. But the general point is still valid. Any "unemployment" would mean that all the necessary work was done and the people who recently became unemployed would be taken care of while they were waiting for more tasks to come up. Most likely, they would soon start helping out in some other way or simply enjoy their free time. In a healthy society, everyone would enjoy plenty of free time.

In our world right now, there are plenty of unemployed people with excellent skills. Take construction workers, for example. Our infrastructure could be greatly improved and this work would bring many benefits to our entire nation for a long time to come. These people can do this work but the jobs have not been funded so they are unemployed. You hear about this kind of thing all the time. "Oh, that's a good idea but there just isn't any money for it." Ah, come on now. Would that stop the indigenous people? Can you imagine this situation: Well, we are all hungry, and even though there is plenty of fertile land, there isn't any money to pay our farmers so it looks like we will all just have to starve. Ridiculous.

Yes, of course, I am again oversimplifying but some of these ideas are worth contemplating. And, by the way, I think it would be good to create the money and pay the construction workers to improve our infrastructure. This money should be created and *spent* into the economy, not injected into the economy as a loan. (It should be *spent*, not *lent*.) This money would then go into free circulation because the workers would spend it on food, cars, houses and so forth, and then it would move on from there.

While I think that this money should be created now for this purpose, I also think that money should only be created in a responsible way. If the government's central bank just created money in wild excess for unnecessary things that do not benefit the entire nation, the value of the money would be diluted unnecessarily. While that is indeed happening to some extent today, this problem is compounded because of two factors. One, while the central bank is supposedly a government entity, in practice, its assets are to a great extent privately controlled and this private group is greedy beyond measure. Two, the money that is being created is being injected into the system as a loan, and the taxpayers are on the hook for both the principle and the interest.

When money is created out of nothing, nothing should be repaid. It's as simple as that. Keep in mind that there are times when the government should be allowed to borrow money that already exists from people, corporations and even other countries and that money should be repaid with interest. But when money is created out of nothing, well, nothing should be returned.

So what can we do today within the confines of our modern economic system to make things better? Perhaps we should consider bringing more democracy into the workplace. I have always considered it odd that we are continually told that we live in a free country, and yet as soon as we arrive at work, it basically looks like a dictatorship.

What about giving a democratic voice to each and every worker regarding all the things that affect them? This would include pay, working conditions, and most importantly, what is done with the profits that their work creates. When workers have both a voice and some ownership, we have a worker owned cooperative. Co-ops are not a new idea and certainly they are not the answer to all of our economic problems but they seem like a step in the right direction. Surely the workers will not vote for things that damage their community, right? There have been plenty of successful co-ops in America, Europe and elsewhere so maybe we should create more of them.

While I do find the economy interesting, it is not what I want to focus on since it is just an outer manifestation of the core beliefs of our society. Both the group as a whole and each person individually are creating their particular experience as a reflection of their core beliefs via the principles that we discussed in the last chapter.

So let's put the economy aside and take a look at the fundamental "fork in the road" concerning our shift from the world we have now to a world of peace.

Our Shift from Competition to Cooperation

As you know, there are healthy fears and unhealthy fears. A healthy fear will arise when there is a clear and present danger, and your body and mind will react immediately in a natural way to protect you as much as possible from that danger, and the situation will play itself out fairly quickly. This type of fear does not occur very often and therefore cannot lead to a state of constant fear.

Unhealthy fears are imagined or exaggerated fears about the future and they can lead to a constant state of fear. Yet the mind and body do not have an available course of action to protect you. Because of this, these constant, vague fears can lead to mental, emotional and physical problems. How many people do you know who simply worry about not being able to keep up with everything or fill their day with other stressful concerns?

It is important to note that anxiety, stress and worry – which are all dull, drawn-out fears – can only arise from unhealthy beliefs about what might happen; they do not arise in response to what is actually present now. As I mentioned in an earlier chapter, at the deepest level, only false beliefs can prevent you from being at peace.

In today's world, these unhealthy fears have spread throughout society to the point where we have created a fear-based society. When I first heard that phrase decades ago, I did not fully understand its depth. I thought that it just meant that there was a lot of fear in our world. Now I believe that I see things more clearly. The very foundation of our society is based on unhealthy beliefs that are permeated with fear. This makes it much more likely that people born into our society will adopt these unhealthy beliefs. So this circle feeds back on itself and it can be quite challenging for anyone to break out of it.

This is very much like being hypnotized with the additional effect that you then continue to hypnotize yourself!

All of this has fragmented our society to the point where everyone is simply watching out for themselves. Just look at the phrases that we ourselves use to describe our own society: keeping up with the Joneses, every man for himself, the rat race, a dog eat dog world (boy, that one is really graphic) and the list just keeps on going.

We have lost the vital fundamental supporting cooperation of the group and replaced it with the struggle of the individual. It's like everyone has been exiled from the group.

As you know, some indigenous people exiled individuals for extremely disharmonious behavior and this was often a death sentence since it is difficult for a single individual to provide everything that he or she needs. But when our society shifted to an "every man for himself" social structure, it became as if everyone was exiled from the group, and the true unification of the group was destroyed.

In a strange way, though, this "un-unified" group is still viable enough to survive to some extent, although not too peacefully. Instead of being condemned to death by exile, we are individually pushed towards a life of competition. We start to compete at a young age in order to win friends and get better grades in school. Then the competition continues for the best colleges, jobs and spouses. This competition is not harmonious and when it spreads throughout the many nations of the world, this disharmony comes forth in war.

Competition can only lead to war because each step along the path is a little war.

Yet when we cooperate with one another by putting our values of caring and sharing into action, we enhance the well-being of all the individuals in the group while also enhancing the vitality of the group itself. This is true even though it is strongly refuted by those who support competitive social systems. Indeed, it is only cooperation, not competition, that can give us outer peace. And this can only come when we as individuals give ourselves inner peace. The gift of peace is a gift we give to both ourselves as individuals and to ourselves as a group.

Please note that this shift into cooperation does not require that anyone become enlightened. Individually, all it takes is the recognition that cooperation is much more functional and productive than competition, with the added benefit of also being way more fun. And while it would be nice to have most people adopt this attitude right away, the truth of the matter is that you can adopt it right now no matter what anyone else is doing. How 'bout that? And when you do, you just might inspire others to do likewise.

Whatever you are naturally drawn to do is what you add to the mix. You do this without losing sight of what you require for yourself in a wholesome way. You certainly don't need to sacrifice yourself as a martyr. Trust that our human nature is naturally loving and kind; we are not naturally selfish or fearful. If you are pretty happy, loving and peaceful most of the time, then you are getting the job done beautifully!

The greatest gift that you can give yourself is also the greatest gift you can give the world: Just be your natural self.

Now it is of course important that we correctly assess our situation and do our best to solve our challenging problems. It seems to me that humankind is indeed dealing with tremendous challenges on a global scale. Many of our activities are not only fundamentally unsustainable, they appear to be at or close to the breaking point right now. In fact, some people argue that in certain areas, we are already past the breaking point and all the dominoes are beginning to fall.

But I think we should stay positive in our beliefs, emotions and actions. We should stay open to dramatic and positive changes that might be completely beyond what we can imagine. And they might be just around the corner.

Consider the circumstances of an unhatched chick. Imagine that it is you who are confined to the tiny space of the egg. Obviously, since you are the only one in the egg, it is natural for you to focus on yourself. Each day, some of the food is absorbed but no new food is ever delivered. As the supply of food is about to be exhausted, you think that you are surely doomed.

But you have overlooked something. You have overlooked the changes that have been happening to you. You are now strong enough to break out of the shell and into a whole new world that you never could have even imagined – a world filled with other chicks and chickens, plenty of room to roam, blue sky and lots of food! You have entered a world where you are now naturally doing your part by simply being yourself. While this looks radically different from when you were inside the egg, we should not overlook the fact that you were naturally doing your part then, too.

We all have magnificent opportunities before us and this shift is one of the most fruitful shifts awaiting us now, both as individuals and as a group. When we all sing out in unison, *"One for all and all for one!"* we will all live in peace.

So will we soon break out of our shell of competition and be reborn into a peaceful world that is naturally united in loving cooperation? Well, I don't know, but I do think that it will happen eventually. But knowing when is not important. The only thing that is important for me is to cultivate and maintain a personal state of peace, love and joy, as best I can, while being active in the world, in my own unique way.

A world without war is built by people with peace in their hearts.

It is in this context that I hope to inspire you to put mystical optimism and your values of caring and sharing into action at every moment. Work towards a more desirable future in every way that appeals to you. Do so joyfully with hope in your heart and without fear of what might arise.

And of course, in a book whose primary focus is the discovery that there is only the One True Self that arises as all apparent selves, I must point out that competition and cooperation both come forth from the One Divine Will and this leaves us nothing at all to worry about.

When we celebrate both our divine uniqueness in form and our divine unity as Source-Awareness, we find the deepest inspiration that opens up our loving hearts to everyOne. It is only through the many that we can share the One Love of God.

While it is not our nature to know what will arise next on the physical plane, we can glow with the flow and dance with the divine in a way that allows us to experience the deepest richness that life has to offer, no matter what shows up!

Yes, embrace the whole of life and
you will embrace the whole of God!

~~~ * * * ~~~

This would usually be called "The End"
but let's instead call it "A New Beginning."

I want to extend a very warm invitation for you to interact with me. This wisdom unfolds more freely and completely when there is a dynamic, two-way conversation so please don't be shy about getting in touch through my website.

In truth, I honor your divine nature, Thomas Razzeto

Afterword – Two essays from my website

I have decided to include the following two essays in this book even though they are redundant. If you have already read the book, you will recognize much of this material. But perhaps these concise presentations will bring you even more clarity.

The Loving Heart of Enlightenment

This is a summary overview of spiritual awakening in simple, clear English.

You know you exist. This, of course, is obvious. And you know you are sentient. This, too, is obvious. These two points, taken together, lead to a very interesting question. Could it be true that you exist fundamentally – and by that phrase, I mean what you really are when stripped of everything that is not essential – could it be true that you exist fundamentally as this power of sentience, as this open capacity for experience? In other words, could your fundamental identity be pure awareness?

Now I use this word "awareness" a lot, so I want to be clear right up front that I am not using it in any special way. It just means the power of sentience. Yet I use this phrase "pure awareness" to emphasize the idea that this awareness is not a thing.

You are not a thing that is sentient. You are not an object that is aware. You are not a sentient being. *You are sentience itself.*

Now when I say that this awareness is not a thing, I mean that it has no thing-like qualities that can be perceived in any way whatsoever. This awareness perceives, but it cannot be perceived. This paradox was spoken about rather poetically by some of our most ancient texts – oral texts that go back almost three thousand years, the Upanishads.

They offer us this: "This awareness is the unseen seer of seeing, the unheard hearer of hearing, the unfelt feeler of feeling." And it goes on. To what these texts offer us, I like to add my own thoughts: This awareness is the undreamt dreamer of dreams.

The idea that you exist fundamentally as pure awareness is the third way that you can identify yourself. You already know the first two ways yet I still want to put them on the table for completeness. So here they are.

The first perspective offers us the idea that you exist fundamentally as your body. And when your body dies, that, my friends – according to this view – is the end of you.

You might be surprised to hear me say that there are two things about this perspective that I really like. The first is that it highly motivates you to take care of your body in a practical way, and I think that's a good thing. The second is that this perspective does not really answer all of our deep questions about life and creation and so forth, so it leaves you plenty of room to stand in wonder and awe of the world that is all around you. I think this is profound, beautiful, important … and fun! Now, these two points actually apply to all three ways that you can identify yourself, and I just wanted to mention that.

Now, in my opinion, the idea that you exist fundamentally as your body is best described as incomplete rather than wrong and this leads us to the second perspective, which offers us the idea that you exist fundamentally as your soul, which associates with your body. And yet again, in my opinion, this perspective is best described as incomplete rather than wrong.

The third perspective, which again, offers us the idea that you exist fundamentally as pure awareness, comes about, not through observation and logic, but instead, through a spiritual, intuitive awakening. And to be more precise, there are three key awakenings regarding this awareness. These awakenings can occur in any order or in any combination, including all at once. So in my presentation here, when I say first, second and third, I am only talking about their order in this presentation, and not necessarily the order that they will occur for you.

The first awakening is the one that I've already touched upon several times: "Ah, I am not *fundamentally* my body, and I am not even *fundamentally* my soul. Instead, *I am fundamentally pure awareness!*" That's the first awakening.

The second awakening is this: "Ah, the awareness that's looking out of my eyes is the same awareness that's looking out of your eyes ... and his eyes ... and her eyes ... and the eyes of every sentient being on all the worlds, both physical and spiritual. *There is only one awareness.*"

Now, when I use this phrase "one awareness," it's not because you can see it and count it, because as I mentioned earlier, this awareness is completely imperceptible in every way. So instead, we use this phrase "one awareness" to emphasize the idea of wholeness.

This awareness never breaks itself into pieces, whether those pieces are disconnected or connected. Furthermore, this awareness is not like a tree with a trunk of the one awareness that grows into a branch of your awareness, and into a different branch of his awareness, and into a different branch of her awareness and so forth. No, this awareness never branches out at all. This awareness is always whole.

There is only one Awareness. That's the second awakening.

Now, quickly, before we get to the third awakening, I just want to mention that we call these awakenings "awakenings" since they seem to happen suddenly and yet they are never instantly complete, just like waking up in the morning. These spiritual awakenings always have a period of deepening, and this deepening can last years or even lifetimes. During this time, these concepts are transformed from mere ideas into a living truth that burns within your soul.

Now, here's the third awakening. *This awareness arises as each and every thing that it is aware of.*

What we are talking about here is God and creation – Awareness (God) and the objects of awareness (creation). It is very simple. When I use this phrase "objects of awareness," I am talking about anything at all that can be perceived in any way at all. So I am not just talking about physical objects, I am also talking about thoughts, emotions, nighttime dreams, intuitive feelings, energy states, hallucinations – anything at all that can be perceived in any way at all is an object of awareness.

Now, with this particular awakening, we recognize the second capacity of this awareness. This awareness has both *the capacity to perceive* and *the capacity to create what it perceives*. This process of creation is best described as an emanation – a spontaneous emanation – and this Awareness is the source of this emanation. This is why my mentor, Timothy Conway, and I refer to this awareness as "Source-Awareness."

This Source-Awareness spontaneously emanates as the totality of created reality and this Source-Awareness is what you truly are fundamental. This Source-Awareness is looking out of your eyes right now!

Not a piece of it. Not a branch of it. The wholeness of this Source-Awareness is looking out of your eyes right now!

There is an ancient metaphor that will help us here. It is the metaphor of the actor and the character. So just think of a Hollywood actor and when you do, it's easy to see that the actor is the source of the character. Surely it's not the other way around. The character is not the source of the actor. Furthermore, the character cannot go on the stage without the actor. And yet, the actor can drop the role of the character at any time. Because of this, it is wise to make a distinction between the *transcendent source* (the actor) and the *dependent construction* (the character).

And yet *when* the actor comes forward as the character, they are one. If you are standing in front of the character and you want to find the actor, you do not need to dig into a deeper and deeper layer. No. When you look into the eyes of the character, you are looking directly into the eyes of the actor. They are one.

Of course you see what this metaphor is pointing to. This Source-Awareness is the one *invisible* Actor who arises as each and every *visible* character, as each and every *visible* person. It is God who is arising as everyOne and it is God who is doing everything.

We have all heard it said, "We are all one." Yes. Yes, of course. But this brief statement is a bit more confusing than it needs to be. It starts off by speaking from one perspective and then it changes to a completely different perspective and it doesn't even give you a hint that it's going to do that. So I like to add a few words. Not too many. And here they are: "In form ..." (meaning "in construction," "in creation," "in the world all around us.")

"In form, we are many; in essence, we are one."

In this, we see that it is only through the many that we can share the One Love of God. When you look into the eyes of another, you are looking directly into the eyes of God. It is God who plants a seed in your soul that grows into the loving heart of enlightenment.

~~~ * ~~~

Anatta – "Not Self" Rather Than "No Self"

Today I am going to talk about the word "anatta," which in my opinion is best translated as "not self" rather than "no self," which is fairly common. This is a very Buddhist topic and my mentor, Timothy Conway, is an expert on Buddhism so I learned this translation from him.

I think a good place to start our exploration of this subject is to consider the context in which the word "anatta" was originally used. This takes us back two and a half thousand years to texts in which we find Buddha contemplating the five components of the person – the five "skandhas."

For the purpose of today's talk, we don't even need to go into the details of what those components actually are. All we really need to do is notice that Buddha is going through the process of disidentification. He considers each component individually, and then for each one, he repeats: "This is not mine. This is not who I am. This is not my Self." And Timothy clarifies that "my Self" means the "True Self."

I think it can be helpful to add the word "fundamental." This is not my *fundamental* Self. And this brings up a good question. What is your fundamental self? What is your true identity?

Well, as you may know from my other talks, I offer the idea that you exist fundamentally as pure awareness, the One

Divine Awareness. This is what you are fundamentally. *This is all you are fundamentally.*

And yet there's more to what you are – but none of that is essential to what you are as pure Awareness. Through the miracle of creation, this formless Awareness paradoxically arises as the form we see all around us. And this is what you are in a nonfundamental way.

To help us understand this point a little better, let's briefly consider the metaphor of the actor and the character. This will be very quick. When the actor comes forward as the character, they are one. That's an important point. And yet, the character is not fundamentally who the actor really is. The character is not essential to the actor since the actor can drop the role of the character at any time. The actor arising as the character is very much like God arising as creation so I hope you enjoy pondering this metaphor.

Now, let's get back to the process of disidentification. This process is not really complete until you clearly recognize that you exist fundamentally as pure awareness. Then this wisdom deepens and you also recognize that there is only one Awareness which arises as everyone. Remarkably and paradoxically, everyone is a unique expression of this one changeless Source-Awareness. In form, we are many; in essence, we are One. The recognition of this is the process of reidentification.

So first, you disidentify from the person while clearly identifying as Source-Awareness. And then you reidentify in a profound and yet nonfundamental way as everyone, including the person you appear to be.

So you disidentify from the small and reidentify as the All.

This reidentification is the source of the deepest inspiration for kindness and compassion. You love everyone, including yourself, because everyone is fully divine in both their essence and their form. This is why every time the subject of disidentification came up in satsang with Timothy, he always made sure to also talk about this process of reidentification. This is what opens up the loving heart of enlightenment, so you see why it is so important.

Now, let's get back to the word "anatta" and this time, let's translate it as "no self," as in "no self whatsoever." And let's also completely remove the word "anatta" from the context of the process of disidentification. So now we have this simple statement: There is no self. But that's basically saying that you have no identity. And that's the same as saying you do not exist. But you know you exist. This is self-evident. The real question is: What is it that you exist as?

As you as already know, I offer the idea that you exist fundamentally as pure Awareness. This Awareness is the open capacity for experience that you intuitively know yourself to be. Now, I also offer the idea that you exist in a nonfundamental way as all of creation – as everything that can be experienced. So this idea that you do not exist is merely a misunderstanding that comes about through the mistranslation of this word "anatta."

Another expression that comes about through this same mistranslation goes something like this: "there are no persons" or "the person does not exist." Well, just because the person does not exist *as your true, fundamental self* does not mean that the person does not exist. When we look around, we see many persons, so clearly they exist. I think that the true teaching is that the person exists as the character, not the actor. The person is not who you are fundamentally, that's all.

Now the last expression that I'll touch on today goes like this: There is no one here. Ah, but surely someone is here. God is here! God is the One who is arising as everyone. I love that word "everyone." Sometimes I spell it with a capital "O" in the middle to help people see that God is "in" everyOne.

When we celebrate God arising as everyOne and everything, and also celebrate this formless Source-Awareness, we celebrate the totality of Reality. This is what the Hindu tradition so wisely points to with the following two phrases. The first is "Nirguna Brahman," which means "Reality without qualities" – Source-Awareness, completely formless, completely imperceptible. And the second phrase is "Saguna Brahman," which means "Reality with qualities" – all of creation, and yet, still the same Reality. God and creation are One Reality, not two. This is why we use the word "nondual." This is the deepest core idea pointed to by our ancient nondual wisdom.

So now you see why it is so important to contemplate the word "anatta" within its original context of this process of disidentification and to correctly translate it as "not self" rather than "no self."

So here's the takeaway:

Your *fundamental identity* is the One Actor, this uncreated, formless Divine Essence, Source-Awareness.

Your *nonfundamental identity* is the totality of created reality: the stage, the props and all the characters. This is what you are through the process of creation.

And your *functional identity* is the combination of the One Actor and the single character (this person) you appear to be. All of this is thoroughly divine since God is not merely infinitely intimate with all of creation, God *is* creation.

It is God who is arising as everyOne and it is God who is doing everything. How wondrous!

~~~ * ~~~

Thanks for reading my book!

I hope you found it to be not only inspirational, but also transformational. While I do enjoy it when people tell me that they find my work inspirational, the main reason that I write is to help people awaken to their true identity as this Divine Source-Awareness. But of course, this is done by God through Thomas; Thomas the person does nothing.

Please write a review on Amazon

If you like the book, please write a review on Amazon. You can't imagine how important this is! And a short review might be even better than a long review. You don't need to buy the book on Amazon in order to write a review but if you do, the review will have the phrase "Verified Purchase" at the top of the review and that adds credibility.

Be sure to mention my full name and the complete title of my book in the review. This is for Google and the other search engines. If you feel comfortable mentioning another popular book, that will help Google and Amazon associate the two books. Maybe you could say something like this: While I really enjoyed (pick your own favorite famous author's book), I also found Thomas Razzeto's *Living the Paradox of Enlightenment* to be (add your comments here). It helps to use the full name of both books and the full name of the authors.

It would also help if your review mentions that it is very easy for readers to interact with me directly.

Thanks again for reading my book!

Thomas Razzeto
infinitelymystical.com

Suggested links, books and audio files:

My essay, "The Seven Key Spiritual Awakenings," and many other free essays on my website: infinitelymystical.com

Timothy Conway's free website: Enlightened-Spirituality.org

If you enjoy listening, I recommend over 75 hours of free recordings of many of Timothy's weekly satsangs. These are mp3 files that you can listen to on your smartphone, tablet, or computer. The link is on my website under "My mentor."

These two books: *The Nature of Personal Reality* and *The Individual and the Nature of Mass Events* by Seth as channeled by Jane Roberts

These two books: *Conscious Life* and *Whatever Happened To Divine Grace?* by Alexander as channeled by Ramon Stevens

The Afterlife Experiments by Dr. Gary Schwartz

Children's Past Lives and Return from Heaven by Carol Bowman

Life Before Life by Dr. Jim Tucker

Robert Monroe's three books on the out-of-body experience: *Journeys Out of the Body*, *Far Journey* and *Ultimate Journey*

Dr. Jeff Long's Near Death Experience Research Foundation: nderf.org

Pollyanna by Eleanor Porter is available for free online

The Happiness Advantage by Shawn Achor

Bashar is channeled by Darryl Anka. See bashar.org.

Why did I not list any books about nonduality? Because I simply am not familiar with any of them. Mine is the only one that I've read. Timothy recommends the book about Ramana Maharshi titled *Day by Day with Bhagavan.* You can read it online for free. He also likes *I Am That*, which is an edited translation of some of Nisargadatta's talks. I think that I would probably enjoy both books but for whatever reason, I simply have not read them.

About the Author

Thomas Razzeto is one of the freshest voices offering some of the clearest guidance on enlightenment, personal peace and conscious creation. He reveals this deep wisdom in simple, clear English so you can easily change your life in a profound way.

Thomas is also a very engaging speaker and was featured twice on the very popular radio show, *Coast to Coast AM*. He has been a guest on Rick Archer's podcast, *Buddha at the Gas Pump,* and even spoke in the prestigious Santa Barbara lecture series, *Mind and Supermind*. Graham Hancock twice selected Thomas as his Author of the Month.

You can find all of his heart-felt and easy-to-read essays at infinitelymystical.com.

Thomas likes to communicate with his reader so if you are inspired, feel free to get in touch with him through his website.

Thomas Razzeto

Made in the USA
Middletown, DE
19 July 2021